SHELTER FROM THE STORM

A Sailor's Life of Havens, High Seas, and Discovery

June Cameron

Heritage
House

Copyright © 2001 June Cameron

National Library of Canada cataloguing in publication data

Cameron, June, 1929-
    Shelter from the storm

    Includes index.
    ISBN 1-894384-21-0

    1. Cameron, June 1929-   . 2. Sailing—British Columbia—
Pacific Coast. 3. Pacific Coast (B.C.)—Biography. I. Title.

FC3845.P2Z49 2001   971.1'104'092   C2001-910493-6
F1089.P2C363 2001

First edition 2001

Heritage House acknowledges the financial support of the
Government of Canada through the Book Publishing Industry
Development Program (BPIDP) for our publishing activities. Heritage
House also acknowledges the support of the British Columbia Arts
Council.

Cover design and layout by Darlene Nickull
Edited by Audrey McClellan

HERITAGE HOUSE PUBLISHING COMPANY LTD.
Unit #108 - 17665 66 A Ave., Surrey, B.C. V3S 2A7

Printed in Canada

The Canada Council | Le Conseil des Arts
for the Arts | du Canada

To my son Alan Douglas Cameron,
without whose help and courage
I would not have begun this adventure.

Contents

Foreword 7

Introduction 9

Bumbling Upcoast 11

This Boat was Made for Racing 28

Becoming a Skipper 39

Chasing Trophies 54

Expanding Horizons 66

Circumnavigation Time 80

Venturing North 118

Dog Days 154

Doing the Johnstone 175

Passing the Cape 188

Glossary of Sailing Terms
According to June 222

Photo Credits 226

Acknowledgements 227

Bibliography 229

Index 231

Foreword

June Cameron will almost certainly chuckle at the thought, but when I began editing her work at *Pacific Yachting* magazine nearly a decade ago she seemed just a bit larger than life to me. Her adventures—and successes—with her all-female crew in the boys' own world of sailboat racing had won her some local fame and inspired at least a few other women to try their hands as well. Her articles for *Pacific Yachting* about her explorations off the beaten coastal cruising track were uncommonly well written and witty. The personality behind the writing sounded adventurous, sharp-minded, occasionally sharp-tongued; she had wide experience and knowledge of the coast and its past. And she illustrated her articles with her own watercolours, too. One of those stubborn, resourceful B.C. coast characters, I thought with admiration.

So I was thrilled when June appeared at *Pacific Yachting* with a delightful article based on her memories of the Refuge Cove of her childhood in the 1930s and '40s. It was an excerpt from her manuscript for *Destination Cortez Island*, her first book, and it seemed to explain everything. She *was* an old coastal hand—she'd grown up on the old coast, on its floats, its boats, and its waters. No wonder the voice in her articles had such an authentic ring.

I was pleased when she found a publisher for *Destination Cortez Island*, and I read it eagerly when it landed on my desk. To my surprise, it changed my view of June in a dramatic way. For *Destination Cortez Island* was really two books. Mostly, it was a colourful, affectionate memoir of a rich time in the life of our coast by someone who had lived it. But it also told a story that was far more complex and bittersweet, of a woman who had moved far away from her beloved coast and its people, raised a family, then suffered personal losses in mid-life—and found herself renewed when she reconnected with her coastal past and the old-timers who had survived all those decades. I enjoyed June's reminiscences of the "old days" around Cortes, but I was moved and inspired by her story of her journey home. Life takes many of us away from places, people, and things we loved, but it's a rare, courageous, and lucky spirit who finds his or her way back.

In a way, *Shelter From The Storm* carries on both of those threads from June's first book. It describes precisely *how* she found her way back: by buying a sailboat and teaching herself first to sail it, then to race it with her female crew, and finally to handle it by herself. This last step set her free to rediscover the parts of the coast she missed and to discover the corners that few pleasure boaters know even today. But this book is also about how June found the courage that I so admired, that made her seem larger than life—the courage to dream about what was up the next channel or around the next point, and to follow her dreams whether they led around that next headland or back to her own past. It's a great story, and as always, June tells it well.

Duart Snow

Introduction

There was never a time that I felt afraid while rowing a small boat, and I have rowed many. The first was a waterlogged clinker-built that was tender to my father's cruiser *Loumar*. I moved on to using my brother's fifteen-foot, smoothly planked double-ender, and much later, when fibreglass was invented, I had, among others, a lovely nine-foot Davidson. I gained confidence during my years of rowboat fishing in the early 1940s around the shores of Cortes Island, one of many islands that clog the British Columbia waterway between Vancouver Island and the mainland. You could start out for a day of trolling in the pre-dawn light with not a ripple on the water and end up fighting large waves as you struggled back to shelter. Your craft would bob and roll about serenely like a floating seagull while you battled to keep the oars from drenching you with spray.

For me, the next logical move was getting a sailboat. But there was a large gap in time between my rowing and my sailing days. During this part of my life I had gone to Normal School, married too young, settled inland at Abbotsford, taught school, raised a family as far as their early teen years, and become a single parent. Buying the sailboat was an act of desperation on my part to help my youngest son and me validate ourselves. And for me it was also almost a return to the security of the womb, for my earliest memories are of waking up in the snug nest of my bunk in our family cruiser.

Not long after getting the boat, I began racing it. To my mind there is no better way to learn how to get a boat moving. There is always another hull similar to yours against which you can compare speed. Every tweak of the sails puts you either ahead of or behind the competition. You go out in a great variety of wind conditions in all types of weather. Cruising folk look at the rain and decide not to get the sails all wet. Racers heave a sigh, pull on their wet-weather gear, go out in the slop, and then haul their spinnaker home to rinse clean of salt and to drape over the shower-curtain rod to dry. We once, rather foolishly, even raced in driving snow, all the while dousing the decks with salt water to stop them from icing up. But summertime was cruising time. The B.C. coastal waters offer limitless adventures, everything from short day-trips to ones that go on for months.

Over the years, when autumn came I found myself more and more reluctant to go ashore, so as a 65th birthday present for myself I traded the sailboat for a diesel-powered cruiser with windows all around and a cozy oil-burning stove. Then I began writing in earnest, and when I wasn't writing about boats I was painting pictures of them. Through my first book, *Destination Cortez Island*, I made new friends who asked about my sailing years, so I settled down to tell what can happen when a middle-aged person runs away to sea. But as the story evolved I realized that what started out as a search for my amniotic home had become much more. What happened while I learned how to sail exceeded my wildest dreams. The experience changed my life.

Bumbling Upcoast

Leaving the wharf near Gibsons Landing at five in the morning to travel 50 miles diagonally across the Strait of Georgia to Hornby Island had seemed like a good idea at the time. As a rank amateur sailor, I figured I could motor quite a bit of the way before the wind arrived. On the coast of British Columbia the summer winds are often lazy and do not get to work until late morning. The weatherman had said there would only be light southeasterlies, so we got up at first light and powered our sailboat out into the strait to find that the report had been correct. After a while, a gentle breeze arrived, so we put up the sails. But as the sun rose, so did the power of the wind. By the time we had put in seven hours of running before a strong southeaster, which pushed us along and included many violent jibes where the boom threatened to rip off the cabin top as it swung across to the opposite side, I began to doubt my judgment in leaving port at all.

The trip was nothing short of awful. As the day wore on, the wind that had plagued us began to die, but now we were being rolled about by strange swells that came at us from the direction of Vancouver Island, cutting in at right angles to the remaining southeast slop as we approached our goal. What was causing this turbulence? No boat had crossed our path to leave its telltale wake.

The answer arrived in a blast of wind that rolled our small sailboat, *Saffron*, right over on its side. Within seconds the snapping sails, writhing lines, and general mayhem had me close to a state of panic. I sent Alan, my agile fourteen-year-old son, forward to gather and bundle the foresail, which I had released from its agony, before I struggled to tip the outboard motor down into the water from its locked-up position. In no time our trim San Juan 24 sailboat turned into a lurching powerboat, with the motor screaming each time it lifted out of the water and gurgling as it plunged back in almost up to its throat. Then, as I turned to drop the mainsail, I saw the rocks of Hornby Reef off our bow.

I pushed the tiller to the right to turn us away from danger, inadvertently relieving the stress on the outboard engine because the hull was now quartering the waves that had rapidly built in size. But without the stabilizing effect of the mainsail we were tossed about in every direction, although we were making headway. (I didn't know that we would have been much safer and more comfortable under shortened sail.) A long heaving tack out to our left and a change in course to the right when we were clear of the southern tip of Hornby soon put us into the blissful shelter of Ford Cove with its already crowded dock.

My exhaustion and relief almost had me crying as hands reached out to take our mooring lines. I'm sure I was babbling about our frightening experience. When the hubbub of docking was finally over I spotted the sailboat that had left us in its wake many hours earlier as we stumbled our way past the southern tip of Lasqueti Island. At the time I had made a mental note to ask the skipper what he did to keep his jib so nicely filled. He had passed us serenely with his sails extending like gull wings on either side. When I tried this, our headsail kept collapsing as it became blanketed by the mainsail, try as I might to have the two balance on either side of the boat. When I eased the nose of the boat around so that the air filled the forward sail, the waves would catch the stern and the wind would fill the wrong side of the mainsail, causing it to backwind enough to send it roaring across to the opposite side of the hull.

After enough of these awesome heart-stoppers I had resorted to zigzagging downwind with both sails on the same side of the boat, which provided us with a faster run over the water but slowed us down considerably as we crisscrossed much of the Strait of Georgia to reach our ultimate objective.

The kindly sailor took me over to his boat and showed me what he called a whisker pole. This was a classy, telescoping aluminum rod with hooks on either end that looked for all the world like a forefinger looping over the end of one's thumb to form a letter D. He showed me how he clipped one end onto a sliding track on the front of his mast and how he hooked the outboard end through the eye of the sail. So that was the secret. He also said that it was possible to tie the boom down to the leeward toe rail of the deck so it couldn't slam across the boat to the opposite side. What he did not explain is that when you use this preventer you'd better not let the wind get behind the sail or the boat will surely be forced over on its side.

On the way back to the boat I stopped to talk to an old fisherman on his troller. I asked him about the powerful wind that had come at us from the Vancouver Island shore. "That were a Qualicum," he replied as he leaned back and took another drag on his greasy, hand-rolled cigarette. "Yuh get 'em just after a sou' easter when she's gonna roll round to bein' a snortin' westerly. And if yuh made it through that wind, yuh'll make it through jest about anythin' the coast'll throw at yuh." That said, he threw his cigarette butt into the sea and turned to resume the splicing job that I had interrupted. I raised my eyebrows at this heartening information, thanked him, and headed back to *Saffron*.

And it did blow overnight, but we were snug in our berths, having put the lion's share of the trip behind us. I lay there and thought back over the past few weeks, amazed at my daring (or was it stupidity?) for exposing my younger son to this risk. We both loved boats and fishing. I had grown up spending every childhood summer on my family's 36-foot cruiser. (This story is told in my book entitled *Destination Cortez Island*.) Alan, as a four- and five-year-old, had put in

A jubilant new boat owner, I try to make sense of a tangle of lines while Saffron *is up on the hoist for a coat of bottom paint.*

two summers on a 22-foot boat that my father had built and helped us convert to a rather cramped but usable craft. We had rolled around in a few sloppy seas and finally decided to put the boat up in the yard and produce our own family sailboat, an Atkin ketch of the Ingrid line. This massive project dominated five years of our life and ended with my husband leaving our three children and me on the shore while he sailed off with a new wife.

I tried to make up this loss to Alan by outfitting our beat-up Sabot dinghy with an outboard. We tented at Smelt Bay on Cortes Island, did a lot of fishing and a bit of sailing, but both of us longed for a real boat. Al wanted to get a commercial cod-fishing vessel, but I could see that this industry was already dying and didn't want him getting caught up in it.

In 1976, by the time he was fourteen, with the help of loans from my father-in-law and my daughter (who happily lent me some of her scholarship money), we began searching for the perfect small sailboat on which to spend our summers fishing and exploring. Specialty Yachts in Vancouver convinced me to take on a golden-coloured San Juan 24 called *Saffron* because, they reasoned, it was one of the hottest little boats in the racing circuit and if I changed my mind I'd have no trouble unloading it. At that time Andy Copeland, the boat dealer, had earned many honours in black *Bagheera*, a sister ship, so I signed the forms, gullibly paying the asking price because I was totally naive (a gross understatement).

A buddy of mine at the time, Mike FitzJames, had bought an old sailboat in Norway in the 1950s. With two crew members he crossed the Atlantic, negotiated the Caribbean maze, traversed the Panama Canal, and ended up in Vancouver. In the 1970s Mike was navigator for a well-respected local racing skipper, Van Leeuwen, when his sailboat nearly won what is known as the Triple Crown in the Vancouver area racing circuit. So he knew a bit about sailing. The week before we were due to head upcoast, Mike offered to take Al and me on a week-

Alan works on boat preparation the first week we owned our treasure.

end training cruise across to the Gulf Islands. He did all the boat handling so I learned little, but we did have fun.

With this enormous amount of knowledge we set out from False Creek in Vancouver, intent on showing our new possession to my parents, who had moved from Cortes Island to Comox when Mother's health began to fail. It was a sunny July day with a typically strong summer northwest wind frothing up the waters of English Bay. I decided to tack my way out along the West Vancouver shore, not realizing that I was working against a strong three-knot tidal flow running into Vancouver's inner harbour.

We tacked interminably, back and forth, back and forth, until we finally rounded Point Atkinson into the more sheltered waters behind Bowen Island. I tried to pump water into a kettle to make a longed-for cup of tea. The pump refused to work; so did the built-in alcohol stove. Al was up top steering and I declared that we were going into

Snug Cove forthwith and if we couldn't fix both the stove and the tap we were taking this damned boat right back. He grinned and said okay (he knew his mother pretty well). Tied up to the dock at Bowen Island we quickly found the press-on clip that held the rubber "leather" onto the pump plunger that served the stove. It was rattling around in the bottom of the cylinder. With the stove problem solved we soon put the water pump to rights and I got my reviving cup of tea. We were committed. (In our years together of maintaining a household without his dad, we had solved many mechanical problems by carefully disassembling and inspecting everything from lawnmower motors to washing machines, so we were carrying on as usual.)

The next morning found us on our way to Gibsons Landing to pick up forgotten items. We tied up at Plumper Cove on nearby Keats Island, the location of many happy family weekends years earlier on our home-built cruiser. I slept uneasily that night, tormented by thoughts of a marriage gone wrong and by apprehension about the long day we were facing tomorrow. But the following night at Ford Cove was filled with blessed relief and total exhaustion.

When we got to Comox we happily tucked our feet under my mother's dining room table. After supper we invited them both for a sail, but Dad declined. My very deaf mother leapt at the chance. Her water years had begun at Lake Winnipeg in 1909 on summer vacations when she was seven. She arrived at Cortes Island as a sixteen-year-old and had virtually lived either on or beside the sea for most of the intervening years. She told us that she had travelled on most kinds of watercraft but had never actually gone sailing.

With Alan steering, we navigated out into Comox Harbour and raised the sails to a gentle evening outflow breeze. In no time Mother took the helm while Al and I did the sail handling. With shining eyes she told us she couldn't remember when she had felt so happy or so at peace with the world. (That evening made the price of the boat worth every penny because she died of bowel cancer the next spring.)

In the morning I borrowed Dad's car and set out to solve the whisker pole problem. In 1976 Comox had little in the way of equipment for sailboats. Certainly the fishing industry was still a major activity, but Vancouver suppliers were meeting most recreational sailing needs. After a fruitless search I went to a lumber yard, bought an eight-foot length of two-inch wooden dowelling, drove a large nail in one end and tied a piece of cord around a groove that I had whittled near the other end, and produced a workable pole. I reasoned that I could insert the nail into the eye of the sail and tie the cord on the other end around the mast—no more accidental jibes for us. It worked!

With renewed spirits we set out for our destination, Cortes Island, pushed along by yet another southeaster. This time we progressed in a stately manner with the genoa poled out to one side and the main boom lashed down to the leeward rail. Before the wind got up too much I was scared out of my smugness when I inadvertently backwinded the mainsail. Oh, oh! The boat was forced around to leeward with the wind heeling us over dangerously. Alan scrambled to untie the knot that restrained the boom. This was one of the many times when his courage saved our bacon.

After that scare, we got along without the preventer. Naturally the wind increased in strength, pushing us through the extensive kelp beds south of Mitlenatch Island, where I realized that my chart-reading skills were just about zilch. Were there any rocks among the tangle? I didn't know the answer to that one so I hung onto the shrouds beside the mast and peered into the depths while Alan handled the tiller, ready to change course. I thanked the Almighty for my years of rowboat fishing, when I had learned to distinguish between surface reflections and underwater shapes.

After tossing our way past the bell buoy that marked the end of the reef at the southwest corner of Cortes Island, we eased into the quieter waters of Smelt Bay and did our first anchoring together. Since the bottom there is sand and mud, it didn't matter that we were still novices at this drill. The anchor obviously held and we climbed down into the dinghy so we could row ashore and tell our friend Nellie Jeffery all about our adventure.

Saffron at anchor, with Al's Sabot dinghy and Seagull engine that he used for early morning fishing trips.

We spent a few days there, sleeping on board at night and renewing old acquaintances as I unwound and adapted to island time. Nellie fed us, let us use her bathtub, and generally cheered me on, as usual.

Cortes had once been home to all my mother's people, though now there remained only my cousins Frank and Bob, sons of my mother's elder brother, Art Hayes. But the southern part of the island was inextricably intertwined with my life. I had spent my childhood summers on our family cruiser at what became known as Cortes Bay. While we were there, we visited my grandparents' homestead opposite the northwest end of the Twin Islands. With my brother George I had walked the trails, explored the beaches, and fished the local waters. My own children had grown to love this paradise because I took them there to visit my parents in their retirement home in Cortes Bay. Now Alan and I were glad to be back in familiar waters, free of land restrictions.

We spent that first summer exploring the local waterways, often tying up at the government dock in Cortes Bay among the fishing trollers that made that safe harbour their summer headquarters. Alan passed many happy hours visiting with the fishermen, who came from all walks of life, while I swam, read, and tried to put my life back together. There was now a marina at what used to be the property of my uncle Dick Finnie, so we could easily get fuel for our many fishing expeditions. With my house rule that the one who cooked the meal didn't have to do the dishes, Al soon learned to make the breakfasts so he could go out fishing in the early morning by himself in our yellow dinghy. I had a small pressure cooker and canned any leftover salmon that we were unable to either eat or give away.

After gingerly flexing our boating muscles for a while, we decided to go exploring. Our first stop was Refuge Cove on Redonda Island, to the east of Cortes. As we left that port late one day, intent on sailing to Melanie Cove, we were passed by what was obviously a racing sailboat. The crew members had their eyes on us as they raised the sails and took off around the corner in a moderate wind. It was apparent that they were challenging our sporty boat to a race. Were they in for a surprise! We struggled along, not sure what to do with the sails as the wind came more and more from behind us. The competition was long since out of sight.

Hours later we approached the area of Prideaux Haven. All I had as a guide was one of the old small-scale charts that showed a narrow entrance coloured in pale blue and crossed with two dotted lines, and another entrance farther along on the other end of Eveleigh Island. This entrance was marked with an X, indicating a rock that appeared to fill the whole passageway. I could not remember how my father had entered this harbour when I was a child, so I opted for the pass without the X. Big mistake.

About an hour before high slack of a very large tide we approached under power with Alan at the helm and me doing the usual figurehead routine. I gasped in horror as rocks appeared on all sides of us. Pointing this way and that we wriggled our way into shelter, much to the entertainment of people enjoying their evening drinks on the decks of ships already there. Once again my guardian angel had come to the rescue. Had we gone aground, the last bit of incoming tide would have lifted us free and we could have backtracked out of there.

Much to my surprise, the harbour appeared to be full. Years before, my father's *Loumar* had been the only boat. We set the anchor near the middle of the larger bay, called Prideaux Haven, because I had completely lost my nerve for trying to get into Melanie Cove.

During the night I sat bolt upright when something thunked into our hull. I lifted the forward hatch and was surprised to find a large powerboat resting against our bow. It became apparent with the breeze hitting my face that a brisk wind was marching up Homfray Channel and had set the bigger boat adrift. I knocked on the hull of the offending boat but could raise no one, so Al got the motor started while I pulled up our anchor and we moved away, leaving them to their fate. In retrospect I probably should have climbed on board and paid out more of their anchor line, but I was too much of a novice myself to take on the responsibility. Morning saw them farther down the bay; apparently their anchor had found something onto which it could hang during the night.

When most of the cruising boats left, we moved our vessel to the small anchorage of Melanie Cove, then rowed ashore and scrambled up the bluff carrying fly-fishing gear in the fond hope that we could find the charted lake. No such luck, although we got a good workout. That evening Al met a girl his age from another boat, so they talked for all hours on our back deck. Having a deaf mother provided Al with distinct advantages for privacy. Without my hearing aid I could only pick up a low mumble.

A southeast wind got up overnight, again setting boats adrift. Three powerboats sharing one anchor and stern-tied to the shore found out that Melanie Cove can be a blow hole, as the wind is deflected by the high local mountains and howls down through what appears to be a sheltered haven.

Intent on having more adventures, we decided to take a look at Theodosia Inlet. My cousin Rod had logged there as a young man and spoke fondly of its beauty. It was still blowing a fair amount as we wiggled through the dogleg that leads to the entrance. Once again my small-scale chart was of little help, so I hung over the bow. The

My painting of an old wooden tugboat leaving
Theodosia Inlet with a boom of logs, c. 1989.

waters were surprisingly clear (I found out later that this is due to the amount of fresh water that flows out of the Theodosia River). In fact, the water was so clear that the bottom seemed too close to our keel. The chart obligingly indicated that there was a rock right in the middle of the channel, so I elected to try for the port side going in. Wrong choice. The push of the current from the river and the wind on our nose made retreat an easy alternative. We anchored in a nearby bay for the night.

I found out years later that a beach extends out from the port side with some rocks here and there, but the channel to the right is deep enough to accommodate the keels of large tugboats. However, the fear generated in me by dodging boulders twice in a row set me back on my heels, so I elected to return to more familiar waters until my sense of adventure was restored.

Next morning found us sailing joyfully up Lewis Channel, which leads around to the "top" of Cortes Island. With the wind on our

Theodosia storm clouds.

tail, the homemade whisker pole came into its own. We burbled past Joyce Point and the entrance to Teakerne Arm, where evergreens climb straight up the high bluffs. The sun gleamed on our sails and sparkled on wavelets, surrounding us in a halo of light. Who could harbour doubts in these conditions?

We anchored for the night by the outfall of the lagoon in Von Donop Inlet, which I had visited many years before as a girl. We decided to explore the lagoon, so rode down the slope in the current in our dinghy, with the British Seagull engine cocked up. I was so naive that I didn't even take a water flask. We explored the rather bleak lagoon with its ghostly clouds of jellyfish and its snag-littered shoreline and then decided that it was high tide so we could exit and return to our boat and supper. No such luck.

We found out that it takes a long time for the waters to pour through a narrow entrance, and the outside waters would have long since begun their retreat before the level of the lagoon equalled that of the inlet. Would these lessons never end? We were finally driven by thirst and hunger to force the dinghy up the tumultuous channel while water still roared into the lagoon. Aside from nicking the propeller on a few rocks and making the engine howl at full throttle, we finally spurted out into the inlet and thankfully boarded our floating home.

The following day we crossed the top of Cortes Island in a lively northwest wind. It was our first beam reach with the wind coming broadside to the hull. Since I had not yet learned that you must ease the lines that control the fullness of the genoa in these conditions, we heeled alarmingly. Before long, water was threatening to come into the cockpit on the leeward side of the hull. We finally gave up sailing and started the trusty outboard engine. At that point it seemed as though I would never learn how to sail.

We tucked in behind the dock at Whaletown and I began to fillet the big rock cod that we had caught before we set sail. I was halfway through the task when a small sport-fishing boat arrived. Out stepped a tall, slim, white-haired man. It was Reverend Rollo Boas, the Columbia Coast Mission minister, who had known my parents and me for years. The mission church and medical clinic were located here, and his arrival should have been no surprise.

As he passed me I scrambled to my feet, fish slime and blood dripping from my hands, and shrieked, "Rollo! It's me. June Griffin." (He would only know me by my maiden name.)

He paused and turned in my direction. "June. What are you doing here?"

"I just bought this sailboat and I'm learning how to handle it with my youngest son, Alan. Al, this is Reverend Boas of the Coast Mission. He knows Grandma and Grandpa."

Rollo stuck out his hand to Al and they barely got two words spoken when I interrupted with a hail of information about our adventures and plans. He listened patiently while my words poured forth, and when I finally paused for breath he asked me what charts I owned. "Mighty few," I replied, and he went back to his boat and returned with chart 3594.

Making the first cut to fillet a rock cod.
Note the heavy glove—those spines can hurt you.

"Here. You're going to need this one if you plan to go any farther upcoast." Since my hands were still a mess, he gave it to Al, who thanked him and unrolled it to have a look.

"Now, June. Why are you hogging all the fun and cleaning the fish?" Rollo said. "Why don't you let your son do that?" I couldn't think of a good answer to that one, so I stood there dumbstruck. "Come up to the house this evening and have a cup of tea with us. Kay will be glad you're here." He turned to look at his fishing buddies, who were well up the ramp by now. "Oh, oh. I'd better get going. See you tonight." And he hurried after them.

Our supply of clothing was limited to three of everything except underwear and socks. After supper we rummaged around to find clean clothes and tramped off up the road to the house of Boases.

Kay was a fine example of how to age gracefully. (In the year 2000 she was still wafting through life as a cheerful, intelligent 94-year-old.) She retained her youthful figure, and her lively face was topped by a swirl of silver hair. While she made tea, the three of us sat talking in the sitting room. I noticed Rollo look intently at Alan,

*The Whaletown wharf, which has been a busy port since the beginning
of the twentieth century, attracts a motley collection of boats.*

blush, and turn to gaze out the window. Wondering what he had
seen, I turned to inspect my young son's shirt. I thought I'd find it
dirty, but no such luck. He was wearing a T-shirt I had never seen
before, his only clean garment, and the logo on the front consisted
of a floppy-eared mule with the words "Good ass is hard to find"
picked out in glaring yellow letters.

During our visit, talk ranged in many directions. Kay took a shine
to Alan and made me promise not to turn him into a husband
substitute. She reminded me that he needed freedom to grow.

As we were about to leave, Rollo said, "June, when I met you
down at the wharf today you were your father. Now, sitting in my
living room, you are your mother." At that I burst into tears. I had
never liked my father's braggadocio. He perpetually hid the real man
under a barrage of self-aggrandizing words, leaving the sensitive self
hidden from view. My mother, on the other hand, was almost self-
effacing, but she was prepared to let you see into her soul. Now I
began to understand why other boaters had turned away from me at
the dock when I swaggered up and took on my father's persona.

We returned to the boat that night carrying a pot of Kay's blackberry jam for Al and reading material for me. Rollo said I had to deal with who I wanted to become and what I wanted out of life and that I should start by setting long- and short-term goals. I was also to decide what I could do right now to start things happening. The setting of goals had never occurred to me. Goals were things men set. Women just eased through life doing their duty. Obviously I had a lot of thinking to do.

Now when Al went off in the rowboat, fishing, I got out paper and pencil and began my quest for self. But all was not serious introspection. We had an adventure-filled time cruising familiar waters. It was when we ventured into unfamiliar territory that I almost ran us into grief.

We decided we'd try to go through the Yuculta Rapids beside Stuart Island. I thought I had timed our arrival at the entrance to the narrows so that we could go through when the water was still, but found to my shock that it was running fiercely. Fortunately it was holding us back, not driving us in. We swirled in to the government dock at the tip of Stuart Island, jumped off, tied our lines, and stood aghast.

What was happening? More ignorance—that was what was happening. When I shared my concern with the skipper of a nearby sailboat, he hauled out his tide book. "Here's your problem," he said. "You were looking at the height of tide, but what you needed was the current tables in the back of the book." This was more of what we had seen at the salt lagoon in Von Donop when we couldn't get out until long after the tide began to drop. I thanked him and returned thoughtfully to *Saffron*. It was time to admit that I needed to stick to familiar things until I built up a larger store of knowledge.

Bark peeled from arbutus trees and leaves rustled underfoot these days when we walked onshore. The time had come to point the bow downcoast and resume our life in Abbotsford. Not only did I have to return to teaching, but I also had to become a student. The things I learned by osmosis as a child travelling on a boat with my father were obviously not enough to keep us safe. So I registered for Power Squadron courses, which were taught by volunteers who could tell me what I needed to know about chart reading, navigation, and boating.

But the summer had been good to us. Al's teachers asked me what I had done to him. "Last spring he walked along the hall looking down at the floor. Now he looks you in the eye and says 'Hello.' He is not the same person."

Neither, for that matter, was I. And strangely enough, I was no longer afraid of the dark. Perhaps this was because of the goals I had set for myself. Now I knew where I was going.

This Boat was Made for Racing

Back in Abbotsford it seemed that my boating life was going to echo the routine followed by my parents, who used the boat only in the summer and left it idle at the dock for the rest of the year. With my home and job 40 miles inland up the Fraser Valley, it was unlikely I'd opt for an evening's sail. So life became the usual humdrum of work and fall garden clean-up.

I was shaken out of this routine by a phone call one Tuesday evening in October. It was Gerhard Storch, the sailmaker. "June? Storch here. How'd you feel about racing your boat? I've been sailing and racing multihulls and I need practice on a monohull. Since you've got yourself a fast boat in *Saffron*, I'd like to see what we could do with it."

I hemmed and hawed for about five minutes. He said if I agreed he'd have the boat rigged by the following Saturday.

When I arrived at Heather Civic Marina in False Creek, *Saffron* was outfitted with a new spinnaker pole and spinnaker along with a crew of two, Gerry Storch and a friend. I was assigned to work the foredeck. As I had never touched a spinnaker before, this called for a quick immersion course in sail packing and handling. Fortunately for me it was a typical Vancouver light-air day with lots of time for instructions to fly from the cockpit to the bow as I tried to make sense of the tangle of lines.

We raced the boat off and on all winter. I was on a steep learning curve, but Gerry made it fun. He was short, wiry, and amazingly strong. Because his multihulls handled quite differently, he was on a learning curve, too. Sometimes when my little boat surged along under spinnaker, the powerful winter wind snorting out of the east would shift to more abeam and we'd be rolled into a broach, with water tumbling over the toe rail and down into the cockpit. When this happened a huge grin split Gerry's black beard and he'd crow with delight. With a few deft moves he'd have the boat back on its feet again and we'd watch for the next gust. When things went wrong (generally from an error on my part) he never lost his temper. He solved the problem and carried on.

Opportunities for getting into competition were plentiful. The Royal Vancouver Yacht Club (Royal Van) offered both Saturday and Sunday races every other weekend, all winter long. Alternate weeks we could travel out to Fishermans Cove at the entrance to Howe Sound and join in the West Vancouver club races, known for good reason as the Snowflake Series. That was a long haul for us, but the advantages to learning were great. Violent winter outflow winds from Squamish gave us practice in handling the boat in rough water. While the race was on there was no time for chit-chat, but during the two-hour run back to the moorage in False Creek we shared our experiences.

When I asked Gerry if he had always been a sailor, he replied that he had grown up in East Germany, where he had gone mountaineering and also raced his motorcycle, eventually roaring past the guards and through the barricades into the West. When he arrived in B.C. he began whitewater kayaking before that became a popular adrenalin sport. Then he turned to sailing. He loved anything that involved risk. Learning how to sail with someone like this guaranteed that I would feel that near-disasters were all part of the game. There was never anything timid about the enterprise.

That spring, Gerry got me to join the Royal Navy Sailing Association because you cannot enter your boat in races unless you belong to a sailing club that is authorized to put on races. There is no intended snobbery here, just the need to have someone sponsor races. Volunteers do race committee work, but money is needed for equipment. Clubs range all the way from those owning extensive properties, such as the Royal Van, to the Tiddlycove group that owns nothing except the basic equipment needed to run races: start guns and flags, etc. This club exists purely for the joy and camaraderie of racing, and rents meeting halls instead of owning any buildings. In time I joined this lively bunch, but at the beginning of my racing experience I was affiliated with the Navy group, which met down at the base on Discovery Island in Coal Harbour.

I eagerly anticipated the first club sailpast because I had read all about these affairs in boating magazines. I outfitted myself, Al, and my daughter Trudy in white trousers and shirts, and we travelled around from False Creek to Coal Harbour to take part in this annual salute to the club commodore. I hadn't a clue what was expected either of my crew, my boat, or me, and the club executive handed out no information to neophyte members. It turned out to be a most embarrassing day.

First off, I did not know that all the crew must stand rigidly at attention as the skipper returns the commodore's salute while moving sedately past his craft in a single file of boats. I should have known from my student air corps experience during the Second World War that this was the norm, but I somehow did not connect the two events.

When we tied up at the dock later, I assumed that food would miraculously appear in the clubhouse as was the case at the big clubs with meeting rooms. But no, the various wives supplied snacks from the galleys of their boats and I was invited to go on board and join one of these groups. Of course I brought my young people along, but as I passed a tray of food to the back deck where they huddled out of the wind, the hostess snatched it from my hand and put it back on the table. I realize now that the wives were catering to the men, but

I fit neither category. As a woman I should have supplied the food, but as skipper I should have been fed.

We retreated from our first sailpast feeling hungry and negative. I motored the long distance back to our mooring and took the family out to dinner. An unusual end to sailpast day and, needless to say, my young people lacked enthusiasm for future club events. But if I wanted to race my boat I had no choice but to remain with the group, and I gradually learned the rules of behaviour.

When you register with the Pacific Handicap Racing Fleet (PHRF), your boat is assigned racing numbers that your sailmaker glues onto the mainsail so that race committees and other skippers will know the specifications of your craft by looking up its number in the list of boats entered in the roster. Based on various measurements, an estimation is made of the optimum speed your boat should be capable of making if everything is done perfectly, including such variables as speed of sail change and choice of route. The rating assigned to the boat helps your competitors form some idea what to expect of you and your craft, much as a golf handicap gives other golfers an idea of your potential.

Because *Saffron* was a light, fast boat she was expected to make good time, but that depended almost entirely on who was at the helm making the decisions. Since my job with Gerry Storch was managing the foredeck, I had not got into the logistics of the actual process of racing. I came to town, did my job, and went back to Abbotsford to work and run my household. I coasted along in this manner until Gerry dropped a bombshell. "It's time you entered the single-handed race." This race went from Vancouver across to the Vancouver Island shore at Nanaimo on a Saturday in early June, and back on Sunday.

I quailed at the thought and asked, "How on earth did you come up with that idea?"

He said, "You have a great sense of balance, you move about the deck securely, and you know enough about sail handling. Also, the experience will make you a better skipper."

Saffron *beating to weather. The wind bides its time before hitting you with a faceful of spray.*

When I asked how I should go about preparing, he replied that I needed to put in about eighteen hours sailing alone and that I should never leave the safety of the cockpit without first thinking out every step of what I intended to do. In many ways Gerry was like my brother: he assumed I could do anything he did, was totally fearless around the water, and expected me to be the same. Without his steady nudging I would probably never have done the things that I eventually did.

I vividly remember the first time I left the dock alone. With no crew member to remove docking lines and fenders, I motored out into the passageway and put the motor in neutral while I tidied up the decks. False Creek was still a busy waterway for tugs at that time, and a loud toot from one of them brought me briskly to attention. Being both crew member and skipper kept my head swivelling. I had worked up a sweat by the time I had the mainsail raised. Then I carefully threaded the boat out through the opening in the old railway trestle that still stretched across the mouth of False Creek.

The breeze in English Bay was thoughtfully gentle, so I raised the genoa, cut the motor, and put in a short sail while working out the logistics of tacking by myself. I found that I could steer with the tiller between my knees while I put the nose of the boat through the eye of the wind and over onto the other tack. Handling the lines fastened to the headsail proved to be no great problem as long as I had the waiting line at the ready on the winch. But the energy spent on apprehension kept me to a short sail that first day. As I coiled a line during the run back into the harbour, steering with the tiller between my thighs, I glanced down and realized, with a chuckle, that it looked rather like an impressive phallic symbol.

I put in a number of hours doing what an aviator would have called circuits and ricochets before I developed the courage to try to set the spinnaker by myself. I chose a sunny, warm, Sunday afternoon when there was a gentle northwesterly breeze ruffling the waters of English Bay. Spinnaker bags are traditionally clipped onto the bow pulpit with the great triangular sail carefully packed inside and with the three colour-coded corners looking out at you. You have to go forward, attach the line that will pull the peak of the sail to the top of the mast, and then fasten the two lines that lead back through blocks that are located on each side of the stern of your boat. You also have to prepare the pole that holds the windward corner of the sail out from the hull.

All this is done while the mainsail and headsail are moving the boat forward through the water. The idea is to raise the great billowing spinnaker in the shelter of the genoa so that it doesn't fill with air too soon and tangle into an hourglass shape before you have all the cloth out of the bag. I had a line rolled three times around my tiller and clipped from toe rail to toe rail so my boat would maintain a fairly even course while I struggled around up front, because the rules for the single-handed race forbade using any kind of automatic pilot.

The San Juan's hull was narrow at the bow, and when I went forward it mattered a lot where I put my weight. It was a bit like skiing. If I had my weight on the right (starboard) side of the boat it headed off to the opposite side. Ditto with my weight to the left. So it was not just a lesson in how to set a spinnaker, but also in how to adjust my weight so that the boat would maintain an even course.

I attempted to raise that blasted sail four or five times, each time getting something wrong, having to go below and repack, then go forward to refasten. Finally it worked. I lowered the genoa and stood back, tiller between my legs, grinning to myself, when I heard a great cheer. A huge sailboat returning to Royal Van, just down the bay, had paused to watch me in my struggles. The crew and guests who were seated along the top deck cheered and raised their beer bottles in salute, so I clasped my hands over my head and shrieked, "Yahoo!"

In time I acquired a large spinnaker bag that I hooked up in the companionway so that I could douse the sail right into the bag with all the lines still fastened on. This meant I did not have to go forward to prepare the bag nor did I have to repack it. When the sail was down it was already stuffed inside the bag with the corners peeking out. Then I clipped the two spinnaker lines and halyard together and dragged them back around the hull to one side of the stern, well clear of the trailing end of the boom, before going forward to clear away the pole. This idea of moving the bag to a handier spot did not occur to me until after I had done my first single-handed race. We do seem to learn things the hard way.

A few days after my Sunday afternoon with the spinnaker, I got another phone call from Storch. "June, I've found someone to do the Silva Bay Layover race with you."

"What's that?" I asked.

"It's a fun race that goes across the Strait of Georgia to Silva Bay on a Saturday. We have a barbeque that evening on Tugboat Island, the Royal Van outstation, then we race back to Vancouver on Sunday. It'll be good practice for you to get ready for the single-handed race, and Barbara Traill knows her stuff, so she'll be a great crew member for you."

"You mean there'll be just us two women?"

"No problem. Barbara knows what she's doing."

"Oh, great," I said. "It's a good thing somebody does, 'cause I don't."

"Trust me. You'll be fine. Here's her phone number. Give her a call and get organized." And with that he banged the phone down. Wow!

The first time I laid eyes on Barbara was the morning of the race. She was a tall, strong-looking woman with a handsome face and a ready smile. We liked each other right away, which was probably a good thing since our lives would depend on trusting each other.

There was a brisk northwesterly blowing and the trek out to Point Grey bell buoy took much longer than I had anticipated. We arrived too late. The racers were already on their way across the strait. (I was secretly rather relieved because I had been dreading the start without Gerry on the helm.) Since we were loaded with food, sleeping bags, and a change of clothing, we decided to follow along in their wake.

We bashed along interminably. Northwesterlies in the Strait of Georgia can build up a nasty chop, especially if the current flow is in the opposite direction, and *Saffron* was a wet boat. We regularly got facefuls of spray. But the sun was shining and nothing horrible happened, so we pressed on and had lots of time to get to know each other.

Barbara said she had spent her early married years in Vancouver and that her husband was a sailing nut. She had hated racing dinghies in English Bay because she inevitably made some error that caused the boat to capsize—a sure invitation to hypothermia through most of the year. When they were posted to the Caribbean she finally began to enjoy sailing. It was so hot you were glad to fall into the water.

I asked, "How'd you get to meet Gerry?"

"We both raced out of Kitsilano Yacht Club," she said. "Gerry was an absolute demon in a Sabot." I grinned and nodded my head. This was hardly news to me.

The race we were doing was supposed to go from Point Grey to Entrance Island, near Nanaimo, then down the coast to Silva Bay. But with the lousy time we were making and with our late start, we elected to head straight for the finish line. There was no way we would make the cut-off hour if we tried the longer route. Since we hadn't been counted among the starting boats, we were not legally racing anyway, so shortening our course hardly mattered.

When we eventually pulled in to the wharf at Tugboat Island, we were greeted by shouts of welcome from those who had long since finished and were well into their second beers. Apparently we were the first all-female crew to take part in this race (only the committee knew we had cut corners), and in no time at all my boat was completely overloaded with jubilant males. The San Juan has rubber bungs that plug the cockpit drains when you are underway. In the excitement of the arrival I forgot to remove these, but the problem was solved when the boat went so far down into the water that they shot out like corks from champagne.

Gerry was among those who converged on *Saffron*. He brought along Sven Donaldson, who later became a valued friend and racing companion. We enjoyed an evening of conversation and food, although I must admit that the apprehension of the day left me so tired that I excused myself early and fell into my bunk.

I had Barbara guide me at the start next morning. She talked me through it so that I could understand what was happening. I certainly needed to know because the single-handed race was set for a few weeks later.

I first did the single-handed race in 1977, and it was the most exhausting experience of my whole life. I tucked a plastic bag containing snacks and my lunch into the aft lazarette, along with a small pail to serve as a potty. When I reached in to get my lunch, the bag was not there! Fortunately the water bottle was. I settled down to an interminable, hungry, five-hour sail. When I was at my lowest ebb, a seal popped his nose up as if to say, "You are not really alone, June."

Although the race stretched my energy to the limit, the euphoric high on reaching the finish line made it all worth the effort. To top it off, Bob Lefeaux, a great sailor, hauled his blender out onto the dock and proceeded to mix margaritas for all comers. That packed a wallop on an empty stomach! But I was sober enough to see through the ruse when one skipper asked me to come below and help remove a sliver from his finger. It didn't take me long to figure out what sliver he had in mind, and I wasn't about to fall for that one. I had long since made up my mind that I was not going to build my reputation as a capable skipper on my back.

It was not until I returned to Vancouver that I found the soggy lunch. It had jumped over the lip on the floor of the lazarette and had fallen into a well below the back deck, which in turn yielded nine pails of stagnant rain water when I finally pumped it dry. No wonder my boat was stern heavy.

Out of about 63 boats I was fifth from the last, but won the women's trophy anyway as I was the only female in the race. Small honour there. Next year I moved up the list to somewhere near the middle. The third year will always remain in my memory.

The fleet set out across the Strait of Georgia in a southeast breeze in 1979, but as we neared Entrance Island it had died away to a mere breath. I was well up in the pack, behind Bob Lefeaux, when I happened to glance off to my right and saw a squall coming in from the west (shades of rowboat-fishing years when watching the horizon was the path to survival). I hastily doused the spinnaker, put up my medium-sized headsail, and was tying a reef into the main when the wind hit with a surge of power.

I scrambled for the tiller and the boat took off. It was nearly six o'clock by then, when the race is formally ended for that day. My trusty yellow hull roared across the outer harbour and sizzled past the nose of the committee boat to the bang of the gun and a loud cry of "What ho! Well done there!" The guest of honour at this particular race, which is sponsored by the Royal Navy Sailing Association, was none other than the British commodore. I must admit that in a deliberate bit of showing off I had nearly skimmed the paint off the bow of the anchored mark boat, but I think it was the recognition that I was a woman skipper that brought forth the cheer. Only twelve boats completed the race by cut-off time. Although I had been fifth to arrive, my corrected time placed me in ninth spot.

I'm afraid that the balance of the racing fleet was left with half its race discounted, and the fact that I made a rather poor showing the following day against a couple of much younger women in faster, lighter boats did not affect my standing, as it is the total of the two legs that counts. Over the four years that I did that race I moved from the back of the fleet to near the lead, among mostly male sailors, but I never thought of myself as a woman. I was just a person out having fun as I struggled to learn a needed skill.

Becoming a Skipper

Al joined me again for the second summer of cruising. We went back to Desolation Sound, but this time I felt much braver about sailing and navigation. Eventually we built up the nerve to tackle a set of rapids again. There is no way you can leave the waters of the Strait of Georgia without transiting these obstructions, so there we were, tide and current book in hand and heart in mouth. When we arrived at Surge Narrows on a trip to the Octopus Islands, I was nonplussed by the eddies that persisted during what was supposed to be the slack period. Seeking assurance, we stopped in at the government dock on nearby Read Island to ask the storekeeper about the timing. He seemed not in the least surprised to find me skippering the boat, which lead me to suspect he had been at this outpost for a number of years. No doubt he had seen local women running small craft during wartime, when many of the fellows were away.

"These waters are never still, Ma'am," he said. "If they aren't rushing one way they're off on the other. Just trust your current tables. They work. Which is more than you can say for me." We could see by his meagre supplies that he was right. So I bought a few canned goods as a "thank you," and at the next change of flow we were off.

Saffron *anchored in the Octopus Islands.*

When we finally reached the cluster of islands, we couldn't anchor in the tight spots because I didn't own a long floating stern line that would keep us from swinging into the rocks, but friends had told us to worm our way in along the shore near the most southerly island of nearby Waiatt Bay, where we could swing free. Today a commercial seafood farm hogs that location, but in those days we had it to ourselves. An exploration of the islet revealed wild onions growing in profusion. Since the Surge Narrows store lacked this product, I was delighted. Al fished right off a perpendicular bit of ledge and caught a rockfish, so we put together a bouillabaisse with a few clams we found at low tide. Some dried basil, along with the wild, woody onions, provided flavour, while canned tomatoes from the store gave it colour. Oh what bliss, to eat a meal out on the back deck surrounded by the glow of sunset and not another boat in sight.

Once you get to the Octopus Islands you are virtually locked in by rapids. The Okisollos block the passage to Johnstone Strait and the Hole-in-the-Wall stops up the route to the east. We spent a number of days working through these waterways, slowly getting braver. Sometimes, with a big tidal change, the eddies tugged at the keel as though a giant octopus was playing games with our hull. Since the outboard could only push us along at five knots, we didn't linger. These currents could double that speed and we'd be swept along willy-nilly. So we scampered through into quieter water as we searched for good fishing holes.

It took us a while before we ventured through Whiterock Passage. The Surge Narrows storekeeper had assured us that it was navigable but was best done at high water. The current is negligible. The pass appears as a sort of stream that meanders between two rocky beaches. There is a fixed daymark on a rock near the inner end, where you begin with some confidence. You then line up two triangles that are on posts set one back from the other. You can tell when you are on course because they appear as a diamond shape. This leads you almost into the moss on the shore before you turn away. Now you must look behind and line up similar triangles that put you on the path to deep water.

The dogleg itself is free of encumbrances; it just looks awful, surrounded as it is by boulders of varying sizes. Nowadays there are mooring buoys and floats that obstruct anchoring near the entrances. But when we travelled these waters there were no homes nearby, which allowed us to anchor at either end of this constriction and wait out the tide. As to the pass itself, I have seen a sailboat hard aground near the daymark, so it is possible to come to grief.

One morning, after going through the narrows, we were dragging our lure near a rocky point when Al spotted an eagle that seemed to be in trouble. It was thrashing around in the water, struggling to swim ashore, using its huge wings almost as paddles. As we moved closer, the bird finally reached a rocky ledge where it emerged, dripping, with a salmon firmly clutched in its talons. The bird bounced it up away from the water and was settling down to eat when the fish gave a mighty lurch and escaped. The eagle hunched its shoulders, hung its head, and paced around, which prompted us to burst into laughter. It was the epitome of dejection.

Al's kite fortunately landed in the dinghy
when he flew it behind the boat in Calm Channel.

As we left that area to return to familiar water, Al got the idea of trying out the kite that had languished on a shelf. There was a slight breeze, not enough for a good sail, so we motored into it, dragging our yellow dinghy behind. The kite mounted higher and higher as we moved down Calm Channel, but finally a downdraft caught it and it dove into the rowboat, which was certainly a better landing spot than the water. Smart kite.

It seemed odd that I felt able to explore this area of the coast with just my son, but was still apprehensive about racing without an experienced hand on the helm. Perhaps my childhood spent in these coastal waters helped me feel at home. More likely it was the plethora of rules you needed to follow in close encounters with other boats, as well as the turmoil of race starts, that made me cautious. Certainly Gerry Storch had been right. Doing the single-handed race did set me on the path to becoming a better skipper, but when I returned to Vancouver I still felt the need of help in long races.

In the autumn, Gerry suggested that Lorne McGruer might like to skipper my boat. Lorne had recently arrived from Ontario, where he had excelled at racing, as had his brother Colin. Gerry had taken Lorne on at the sail loft, and it wasn't long before I commissioned him to build us a pretty spinnaker so that Gerry could have his "loaner" back.

So Lorne joined the boat, taking over the role of skipper with his capable wife, June Butler, as part of the crew. He handled the boat aggressively. And when we came first a couple of times, I knew my vessel was competitive. At Easter he entered us in the Southern Straits race.

Given our collective lack of local navigation knowledge, I insisted on bringing along my friend Mike FitzJames to fill that role. His experience navigating sailboats in a number of Southern Straits races, as well as his youthful years spent deck-handing on a coastwise fish packer, made him a necessary part of our green crew. Unknown to me, he was short of cash at the time so lacked adequate wet-weather gear and had only socks and running shoes to protect his feet, but he accepted the challenge and showed up for the race anyway. He must have endured agonies. I'm surprised that he didn't just go below and give up when the going got bone-chillingly wet, but he stuck it out, wordlessly fighting hypothermia near the end when Lorne, who was thoroughly exhausted, went below to warm up.

We had a wet run under spinnaker all the way from West Vancouver to Ballenas Island, upcoast from Nanaimo, arriving there near dusk. We dropped the spinnaker and rounded into the teeth of a blustery wind that had us tacking between the maze of islets that litter that waterway and the shore of Vancouver Island. When I went forward to change us to a smaller headsail, I was nearly choked by the stench from a colony of sea lions that nested on one of these rocky outcroppings.

We struggled downcoast until we were finally nearing Nanaimo, when Mike sent me below to confirm the identity of a flashing light on a marker. At that time, although I had taken a Power Squadron

Saffron *shows off her classy new spinnaker*
made by Lorne at Storch Sails.

course, I still had little actual chart-reading experience and couldn't
figure out which light we were seeing. (These navigation tools have a
definite colour of light and flash frequency marked right on the chart
that make nighttime identification foolproof, although in my case
you'd have to admit they were not idiot proof.) In frustration, Mike
roared below, wiped his streaming glasses, and focused the flashlight
on the chart. Right away I was able to see what he meant, but by then
his night vision had been temporarily spoiled. As it happened, we
were in no danger and carried on past Snake Island so that we could

round Entrance Island and begin the long leg home to the finish line at Point Atkinson.

I wish I could report that we did well, but maybe it was enough to have finished considering our lack of practice together as a crew and the general quality of my sail inventory. The result of this poor showing was that Lorne promptly withdrew his offer to race my boat in the Juan de Fuca division of the Swiftsure race that year. Since I was interested in entering that race, which occurs after the Victoria Day holiday in May, Gerry suggested that Sven Donaldson might like to skipper the boat.

This famous event attracts many boats. The race for the large boats is called the Swiftsure and goes all the way out to the entrance of Juan de Fuca Strait, the passageway that marks the western boundary between the United States and Canada. The smaller boats are restricted to sailing out to Clallam Bay on the American shore and returning to Victoria—the Juan de Fuca division. This race offers a wide range of weather and current challenges, with the long Pacific swells providing an added fillip. Skippered by Sven, with Bill Donnelly, Douw Steyn, and me as crew, we entered the race out to Clallam Bay and back. When I asked Bill if he'd like to join the crew, he chuckled that he'd do the race only if we stood some chance of winning. Little did he know how dim that chance was.

Prior to the race we moored the boat at the Royal Navy Sailing Association site near Esquimalt. Sven went out to prepare the boat before the race, removing anything unnecessary that added weight. At the race start line near Brotchie Ledge, outside Victoria Harbour, we milled around for more than two hours, waiting for the westerly to arrive. This waiting can be nerve-wracking as your boat cuts back and forth amid up to a hundred other craft, all trying to stay within reach of the line. The stress made me thirsty so I went below to make a cup of tea, only to find that Sven had removed the tea bags in his enthusiasm about lightening the load. After some good-natured bantering from a passing craft, we were handed a donation of tea bags and I got my cuppa.

The wind arrived with a blast around noon. Since we were in the last class to start (races are divided into classes, with the larger boats going off first), we were pretty well overpowered by the time we reached the area of Race Rocks. When Sven called for a small heavy-weather genoa, he blanched at the sight of the piddling little storm jib I hauled out of the bag. I put the medium-sized sail back on and he worked the boat carefully to weather, luffing the sails each time we were overpowered.

We struggled out to the turning mark and set the spinnaker for the long race back to Victoria. Sometime during the night we had to go onto a port tack so that we didn't end up heading toward the American shore. This entailed my going onto the foredeck, disconnecting the spinnaker pole from the leading edge of the mast, unhooking the other end of it from the spinnaker sheet, forcing the pole to the other side of the boat, and re-attaching the ends of the pole in the opposite way, all in the dark. It was imperative that the skipper gradually turn the boat hull in rhythm with the work I was doing forward, and with an experienced skipper like Sven this all went smoothly.

When I returned to the cockpit, Bill scolded me for going forward without a safety harness attached. I was startled because it never occurred to me to be nervous of falling in, but he reminded me how it would have been impossible for the crew to find me in the dark had I done so. The most useful thing I did after that was to hand up fried egg sandwiches at dawn along with steaming mugs of coffee.

All else I care to say about that race is we had fun and we learned a lot. On my return I immediately commissioned Gerry Storch to make improvements to my sail inventory. I was beginning to find out that this racing game was an expensive hobby. During the early 1980s (when salaries were a lot lower than they are today) it took $5,000 per year to pay the moorage, service the boat, and slowly upgrade the sail inventory. Aside from the new spinnaker, I bought a small heavy-weather jib and, eventually, a good number-one genoa that could hold its shape. Needless to say, Storch Sails made all of them.

Trudy at the helm as we sail to Plumper Cove near Gibsons.

Fortunately it was a small boat. Although I never had money to spend on anything else, I did not care. My boat became my life.

Although Lorne and Sven had done the longer races with me, and Lorne managed the local events, I did attempt a couple of medium-length races with a mixed crew, keeping my boat well out of everyone's way and ending up dead last. But I found that having a male on board tended to put me in a deferential position. Doing the single-handed race in June 1977 gave me the needed confidence to take charge. I signed up for the short races held in English Bay and switched to an all-female crew. My daughter Trudy found women sailors for me among her friends at the University of B.C. (UBC). She had already learned quite a bit about sailing, both with her father on the boat that we had built in our backyard, and with her friend Malcolm Sterling, who had made *Ting*, a handsome ferro-cement sailboat.

One of Trudy's classmates, Michelle James, was the descendant of a long line of sailing liner captains, but she was the only one of her immediate family to love the sport. Michelle taught beginners in small

Enterprise boats at the Jericho sailing centre maintained by UBC. We used to chuckle when she dashed for the opposite rail if the boat lurched. She'd been dunked by so many beginners that she automatically expected the boat to flip over should the pressure of the air be removed from the sails. This sudden righting of the hull often happens at the start line when many boats are milling about. With its heavy lead keel, *Saffron* never dunked her, but it took a while for the conditioning to wear off.

She brought along another of Trudy's classmates, Aldyen Donnelly, who had learned to sail on the boat of her father, Bill Donnelly. We were soon joined by Eleanor Frisk, who often took friends out on her dad's sailboat, which was moored near *Saffron* at Heather Marina. I later added my brother's daughter Sharleen to the group, as she had practically been born on a boat and was fearless. That gave me a pool of talent that collectively knew more than I did.

Our first all-female race began off the pier at Royal Van. The arrival of a small yellow sailboat crewed only by women raised a chorus of hoots, jeers, and silly comments like "What's cooking, girls?" I'm sure the poor deluded males thought we had come to chase them. Little did they know of our determination to succeed.

My only racing starts had been with experienced skippers on the helm, so I aimed at the committee boat end of the line, where they had gone. What I didn't know, as a greenhorn, was that everybody else wanted that space, too, because it gave you the freedom to tack when you chose. Nor did I know that the only boat to legally claim that freedom was the one that could just clear the stern of the committee boat while sailing close-hauled. As it happened, there were two boats on my right who were further outside the rules than I was.

To my left I heard an imperative voice shout at me "Up, up." It was Andy Copeland on his bigger boat. Since I was being pinched in the rapidly diminishing space, I called back, "How in blazes do you expect me to do that?" I heard him chuckle, and then he gave me enough room to squeeze through the gap. Since his company had sold me the boat and he knew I was a greenhorn, he was also aware that we were unlikely to beat him in the race. We struggled around the course, trying to keep out of everybody's way, and finally finished well down the pack.

To help me learn, I studied books. Sometimes it seems that books have helped direct my whole life, whether it was learning how to ski, how to have sex, how to rear children, how to manage finances ... in short, books have helped or hindered all along the way. (In the mid-1950s I even read that vaginal orgasms were the only normal way for a woman to enjoy sex!) I have a vision of myself skiing down the hill of life with an instruction book clutched in my hand.

The good thing about this approach was that I quickly learned the racing rules. The bad thing was that nowhere did it say that beginners would do well to emulate choices made by experienced sailors. When our races went wrong, it was usually because I had gone off on my own personal goose chase.

In the fall of 1978 we stumbled into a race where we did well as an all-woman team—by mistake, as it happened. We had entered the Ballenas Island race. In this event the smaller boats leave the Jericho Beach area, sail to the White Islets near Sechelt, and come back to finish off at the Royal Van dock. If the winds are light this can take all day Saturday, carry on through the night, and end sometime Sunday morning. (There is a 24-hour time limit.) This year the wind was gentle and we sailed along under spinnaker into light air, then into nothing, followed by more spinnaker work as the day wore on. As darkness came, one of the crew discovered the beauty of flushing the toilet when phosphorescence was at its peak. The glowing fluorescent chunks of green light whirled round and round the bowl, and the wake of the boat took on a life of its own. Gentle breezes made it easy for various crew members to try the head and come back chuckling about the experience.

We drifted slowly northwest with the tide, well out in the strait. There was the odd craft here and there, all spread around, but no one seemed to be getting anywhere and the night wore on interminably. We had long since doused the spinnaker as the old southeaster had obviously quit. Our largest headsail was up, but it had been hanging there limply for what seemed like hours. Gradually light puffs of air began to touch my cheek. I shifted the crew to the leeward side of the hull so that gravity would put some shape in both sails, and we began to move toward our objective. I found the wind path to be narrow, and it seemed to be coming at us directly out of Sechelt, but who could argue with that—any helpful breeze would do. A glance around me showed that none of the remaining boats were in our ribbon of air. We took off alone, tacking gently back and forth as we tried to stay in the flow.

We knew we were approaching White Islets not only by the fixed light that sparkled at us, but also by the smell coming from the sea lions roosting there. We spotted boats tucked in the lee of the islets. Keeping our mouths shut, we ghosted along quietly, hoping they wouldn't spot us. As it happened, both Bob Lefeaux and Sven Donaldson had realized that the dying wind could no longer offset the northward pull of the tide, so they had drifted close to shore and managed to hook bottom with their anchors (a completely legal move) while the rest of the fleet drifted inexorably northwest toward Welcome Pass. I later learned that Bob had even caught some fish while he waited for the wind. No removal of tea bags by that skipper.

In spite of our attempt to go quietly through the night, our arrival was spotted. We were greeted with shouts of welcome that alerted everybody to the fact a new wind had arrived along with the crew of women. We slipped around the rocks, carried along by the momentum of our arrival, and as we appeared out on the other side we set the spinnaker, picked up the wind flow, and stuck with it.

A light northwest wind began filling in across the strait and we were gradually joined by the faster boats. This was our first night experience under spinnaker as a crew, so I was reluctant to do any jibing and clung to the original port tack as long as I could. A larger boat came up on us from astern and the skipper made a big to-do about the fact that he was on the starboard tack and I was to yield him the right of way. I said something to the effect of "Don't be silly;

This 1978 Pacific Yatching *photo shows bits of Michelle and Aldyen Donnelly, with June at the tiller and Eleanor at the winch.*

cross behind us" and carried on as I was. I was damned if I knew how I was to go about giving him his right of way and was relieved when he did cross behind. By that time his crew figured out who we were and was most startled to find that they were passing a rank beginner so far into the race.

To prevent any further complaints from overtaking boats, we jibed in our own good time when no one was putting on the pressure. Then we were on starboard and heading away from Bowen Island, more toward Point Grey. This turned out to be most fortuitous because there was a big empty hole in the wind near Bowen Island and the lead boats wisely aimed for Point Grey. I followed them, partly because I was chicken and partly because I didn't know exactly where I was (no long-range navigation [Loran] or global positioning system [GPS] devices in those days to give you your precise location). I was pretty sure they knew where they were, even if I didn't.

At dawn we were approaching Vancouver's outer harbour with the gentle wind keeping steady. There was a particularly big run-in or tide heading east along the West Vancouver shore (shades of my first trip out of the harbour), so I elected to ignore the short trip along Spanish Banks shoreline directly to Royal Van and emulated the few bigger boats that I could see following a triangular course to the finish line. The current swept us toward First Narrows, where we headed off along the Stanley Park shoreline, changed to a genoa, and sailed with the eddy on a quick tack to the finish line. Those who elected to go the short route took five hours to make the distance from Point Grey to Royal Van at Jericho. By choosing the right course we came in third in our class!

Peter Chettleburgh wrote up the report and results of that race in the November 1978 issue of *Pacific Yachting* magazine and included a picture of *Saffron* along with one of Bob Lefeaux's *Bad News*. He and Sven had both won in their divisions. I felt a trifle embarrassed by the results because we had lagged so far behind until well into the race, when the wind god took pity on us and provided that breeze out of Sechelt. I was to use that catabatic wind a number of times in the future as it made an indelible impression, as did the knowledge that a dying wind is usually succeeded by one from the opposite direction.

As you can imagine, at the start line in our next race we were no longer greeted with jeers. Little did they know how limited our knowledge was. But then, boat racing, like many things in life, is partly bluff.

The following January, when the Vancouver Area Racing Council awards banquet for the year 1978 was due to be hosted by Royal Van, I was told to come. Since our list of accomplishments was hardly staggering, I asked, "Why do we need to be there?"

The reply, "Just come, and bring your crew."

During the evening my name was announced and I was presented with a delightful framed cartoon showing my crew and me towing a disabled fishing boat. The title was *All-Girl Boat of the Year*. The crew members joined me at the front for a huge ovation from the gathering. The cartoon was based on a photo that appeared in *Pacific Yachting* magazine, which indeed showed *Saffron* towing a broken-down fishing vessel to the machine shop at Lund. The caption read, "This could happen to you!"

VARC 1978
All Girl Boat of the Year
June Cameron
SAFFRON

Chasing Trophies

Although bay racing is fun, one of the biggest adventures in B.C. coastal racing is the Swiftsure. I had already done the Juan de Fuca division of this event in *Saffron* with Sven Donaldson handling the boat, but I wanted to try it myself. In 1979, after we had two years of racing as an all-woman crew, I felt ready to take it on. To prepare for this adventure, Meg Hill joined the crew. When Meg was married to Gordie Hill, the sailmaker, she was at the helm of their boat whenever they were beating into the wind. This became her specialty. She could make the boat move well in storms and in gentle air. We were lucky to get her as she brought a vast store of knowledge to our crew of neophytes, and during the series of warm-up races in Vancouver, she taught us constantly. She had done a number of Juan de Fuca races and had the added skill of having started out on dinghies. According to Meg, small-boat racing was the best way to learn light-air sailing. Instead of moving the tiller, she first called for the sails to be adjusted as, she said, each time you moved the rudder in light air you were virtually putting on the brakes. Meg took over the upwind legs and brought along her best friend, Karen Renfrew, who also had a lot of experience with small-boat racing.

I sent in the registration fee and got the boat over to Victoria on the long weekend before the race. Crew member Eleanor Frisk was not working at the time, so she went ahead to provision the boat, which was tied up among many other racing boats in Victoria's inner harbour. Race week is an exciting time in Victoria as boats from all over the Pacific Coast of North America come to participate. A stroll around the dock reveals a wide array of innovations designed to get more speed out of a sailboat. There are strict rules governing what is allowable, but sea lawyers always find ways to circumvent these, usually producing a decidedly un-nautical looking vessel, even to the point of eliminating the back wall of a cockpit so that anything dropped on the floor slides aft and is instantly confined to the deep. At major races these inventions are usually kept out of sight until the race starts, for fear someone will copy the strategy, but Victoria races were usually lower key.

Even getting to the race was fun, with many fellow travellers heading the same way. We all caught the Victoria ferry on Friday evening, going by bus or car after rushing away from our jobs on the mainland. We booked in at a hotel near the Parliament Buildings and eventually tried to sleep. Fat chance!

We had a crew of five, which seems a lot on a small boat, but with the extra person there could always be two off-duty except for scrambling from side to side as we tacked. Michelle, Eleanor, and I were from the original crew, but Karen and Meg brought along the knowledge we needed specifically for this race.

As luck would have it, race day dawned with northwest winds screeching down Juan de Fuca Strait. Weather reports had them clocked at 43 knots. While waiting for our turn to start we bobbed and lurched around near Brotchie Ledge, with the genoa jogging up and down on the forestay. I did not know that it should be lashed down because each time the genoa halyard rises it is in danger of jumping the track where it enters the top of the mast. That is what happened to us, so when we pulled on the end of the line to raise the sail, it jammed. Karen immediately offered to go up in the bosun's chair to see what the trouble was. When she reported that all seemed to be clear, we yanked on it. At the time I had no idea that there was

Racing boats cluster in Victoria's inner harbour prior to the Swiftsure.

a considerable gap beside the sheave in the top of the mast. Each time we pulled down on the line, I could see the electric wires inside the mast bulge where they came out at the bottom. I didn't know what was the matter. But one thing was clear: we were without a genoa halyard!

I called a conference. We could abandon the race or we could use the spinnaker halyard to raise the headsail, which meant we'd need to lower the headsail before the spinnaker was set. I had light cotton thread in my emergency supply kit, and I reasoned that I could tie the spinnaker in stops so that it would go to the top of the mast like an inverted Y. Then when we pulled on the sheets the thread would pop and we'd be underway. I had a brand-new, thick, red spinnaker halyard from British Ropes. Given the dreadful strain the wind would put on the rigging, it was probably as well we had a flexible rope instead of steel cable holding the headsail as we elected to go out into that awful weather.

Navigation equipment at that time was rather unsophisticated. We had a compass, echo sounder, marine phone, and a radio direction finder, along with the required safety gear, which included a life raft. The boat was heavily loaded. Small Lorans that gave you a position were just coming into use, but I didn't own one. We used a lot of guesswork to determine our location as currents in that straight passageway bear a heavy influence. In strong winds you keep moving in the right direction, but with light or non-existent air you can spend all night sailing in gentle breezes and actually be going backwards.

Going backwards was not a problem during that race; it was the going up and down that was the challenge. After we passed Race Rocks and got out into the full sweep of wind, the waves grew to growler proportions. Our boat was small and fitted each plane, but going over the crests was a heart-stopping experience. Meg was skilled with the tiller. In order to keep the boat moving smoothly, she wove the hull over the top and down the other side. I think we pounded about three times, and she apologized each time because when you hit down hard it almost stops the boat in its tracks.

As the day wore on, the tops of the waves smoked spume as they were ripped free of the surface by the wind, leaving no whitecaps— just lacy streams of froth and bubbles trailing down the leeward face. Sometimes our eyes could focus on the next swell only as it loomed over us, so that we were either surrounded by water in a deep gully or perched on top where we could see an army of approaching peaks. I think the waves were attuned to the normal rise and fall of the ubiquitous Pacific swells because we didn't actually notice them as you usually do in this area.

At this point we were glad of the extra body on the windward side to help keep the boat as level as possible. With the driven spray and wind it was cold, even though it did not rain. We almost hated it when there was a tack because our bottoms had to warm up a new patch of deck. I was surprised that no one got seasick, but perhaps we were all so busy hanging on that there was no energy left to think about our stomachs. However, all that heaving around and the violence of the wind put colossal strain on the hull and rigging. (More about that later.)

By late day we were approaching Pillar Point, which was easily identified with its turret-like rock formation. The wind was easing off and we put in many tacks trying to get around the cape into Clallam Bay. Experienced skippers likely stay well out in the strait here to avoid the confusion in the winds, which seem to come from a variety of directions. We struggled to get clear and managed to eat a bit of supper between tacks. And we finally began to spot other boats that Meg was able to identify as an array of formidable opponents.

It was dark and the wind was down to about twelve knots by the time we approached the turning vessel, which was anchored in the bay. The convergence of other hulls, shouts, and snapping sails kept us fully occupied while Meg handled the boat. As we rounded the mark we doused the genoa and raised our spinnaker, which was ready in stops. A firm pull on the sheets snapped the soft threads like a row of buttons coming undone, and our beautiful big sail filled with a pop. I took over the tiller while Meg and Karen retired below for a well-earned rest.

I wanted to follow the other boats, which seemed to be heading across for the Vancouver Island shore, but Meg called up that I was to go straight home to Victoria. I think, in retrospect, that the other boats were likely going out to get clear of the muddled air in Clallam Bay. As I tried to go "straight home," we fell into confused air. It took me a while to get clear, but then we were on our way.

My deafness in the higher register makes nighttime communication difficult, as I cannot hear whispers, but I noticed the deep-throated strumming of freighter engines long before they overtook us. By now we were transiting the inbound lanes that carry deep-sea vessels through the strait. Most of them were doubling or tripling our speed, but we tried to give them lots of room. I'm sure their watch captains curse night races, but with their radar they knew far more about us than we did about them.

As we crossed the passageway, trying to get to the shore side of the outbound shipping lane, we began to meet them head-on. This was where I blessed the courses offered by the Power Squadrons.

The lights on freighters are distinctive in that there is a shorter mast in front topped by a white light, and a taller mast aft, similarly equipped. The green and red lights on the right and left sides of the hull respectively give you the information you need about the orientation of that boat to yours. My toes curled up within my deck boots as we scurried to avoid having the lights all equally visible with masthead lights in line. That is no position in which to be! Since we were on converging course, the speed was doubled, theirs added to mine.

We had a memorable encounter with one set of lights. Since we were running at night under spinnaker, changing course was not easy. First we could see both the red and the green, so I headed off quickly to port, then the big boat changed course and we were again in danger of a collision. We did a fast jibe and I dove the other way, and in a few moments we were again seeing both port and starboard lights! When I think back on it, the freighter probably took longer to react to a change of course and was also trying to avoid us. After several games of hide-and-seek, during which time we were converging at about 25 knots, the green light persisted, so I knew we were clear. When the two hulls passed each other we hit the wake almost instantly … too close for comfort altogether.

After all this excitement and stress, dawn came as a welcome sight, chilly as it was. By then we were nearing Race Rocks and elected to go outside them before turning toward Victoria. We doused the spinnaker in order to reach toward the finish. We could see boats ahead working their way past Esquimalt Harbour. They seemed to have sailed fairly close along the shore, then turned and raised their spinnakers for the last leg into the harbour. Our spinnaker was not ready and, frankly, I was too exhausted by then to care, nor did anyone else feel confident about going below to try to prepare it. I should have called Meg to the helm and done the job as I suspect the leading boats were following that course to avoid the opposing currents. As it was, we headed straight for the finish line off Ogden Point.

The gunshot signalling our arrival was a welcome sound. We hugged each other and cheered; then the crew set to work tidying up the boat while I aimed for the inner harbour.

We were not aware that all Victoria knew about our presence in the race. It turned out that when the radio announcer said there was a boat out there skippered by a woman, one of Karen's friends had hastened to inform him that there was not only a female skipper, but that she also had an all-woman crew. Apparently our position was regularly announced as observers spotted us. We had deliberately kept a low profile for two reasons. I never thought of myself as anything more than someone loving to race, and we certainly didn't want attention if we failed to do reasonably well. It would be too embarrassing.

On a race like this, to prevent skippers from jettisoning heavy safety equipment, the committee requires that you pass a safety inspection right *after* you finish. It is the usual pattern to check every tenth boat. I knew this and was grateful to see a boat pulling away from the dock and another one hailed into position. I assumed that we could take our tired, wet selves to the hotel and step into a hot shower. No such luck. There was a reporter on the inspection dock who wanted to get in the first interview. We were signalled to pull alongside.

As you can imagine, I lacked enthusiasm, tired and wet as I was. When the reporter thrust a microphone into my face and asked me what was the most difficult thing about being a woman and doing a race like that, I narrowed my eyes and told him the truth. "It's when you gotta pee." The agony of going below to do that errand, which you put off to the last minute, crashing against bulkheads while you try to unravel the layers of wet-weather gear and sweat-soaked tangles of clothing and somehow manage to find the seat, defies description. I hope he was making a tape recording and we were not actually on the air. I never did find out. But we did pass the inspection, although it seemed that the officials were skeptical that I, a mere woman, could have figured out what we were required to have with us, for they checked everything with minute care.

*We dry out after a very wet 1978 Juan de Fuca race,
where spray was driven by wind of 43 knots.*

We found room at the dock in front of the Empress Hotel, where we hung everything out on the boom and life lines to dry. Nothing in the boat had escaped the damp, and our pretty little craft looked messy and forlorn. It would have to wait there until the next weekend, when we could take it back to Vancouver. None of us had either the energy or the time to do it now. This proved to be an expensive decision, because the city fathers presented me with a large mooring bill. They had tolerated boats being left there prior to the race, but had no sympathy for exhausted sailors after the event.

Calculating finishing honours in those days was a laborious, time-consuming task, different from the situation today, where computers give instant results. Each boat had a rated speed that it was thought to be capable of maintaining if everything went well. The elapsed time set against your ideal time was compared to other boats in your class. We knew it would be hours before our position was known, so we cleaned up, ate, checked out of the hotel, and went our separate ways. I took Eleanor along with me in my car and

SHELTER FROM THE STORM

we drove out to Royal Victoria Yacht Club, which had sponsored the race. I felt wired from lack of sleep.

When the committee found out that we were from the all-female crew, a woman interviewed us. I still was unsure what had happened to our strangled halyard because I had not yet been up to have a look, so I told her that we'd done the race with only one halyard and that when we pulled on the one that was jammed it seemed to be involved somehow with the electrical wires within the mast. The results of her interview, which were included in the book *Swiftsure: The First Fifty Years*, left me sounding like a total airhead. I know she was an experienced sailor, but I couldn't help wondering if she had ever taken her own boat out into such awful conditions with only one halyard and endured the kind of winds we had in such a long race. I sometimes feel that women can be exceptionally intolerant of their own sex. We had raced bravely and innovatively, and as it turned out we came sixth in our class of more than 30 boats.

Of course we would have liked to do better, but I was learning that local knowledge counted for a lot at crucial times in a race. Knowing how mixed up the winds are coming out of Clallam Bay would have helped, as would the knowledge of how to approach Victoria Harbour in adverse current conditions. (Large boats have strategists whose work it is to know these things). However, we did feel satisfaction that we had done the race at all in the gale that developed. We were in nearly the smallest boat and certainly the only one without a spare halyard.

A visit to the mast tower that stood at that time on the north shore of False Creek showed me that the halyard had jumped over the lip of the sheave and was thoroughly jammed. John Timmerman, who also owned a San Juan, told me he had replaced his single loose-fitting wheel with two narrow ones separated by a thin metal plate. This allowed him to have a spare halyard. With this adjustment I would be restricted to wire-to-rope lines as the pulley troughs would be shallow and would never handle anything too thick. But preventing future jams made it well worth the effort.

This was not all that happened to my boat as a result of the beating it took. It was a couple of years before I finally figured out why we were better on one tack than another, no matter how much I tuned the mast by re-adjusting the tension on the shrouds. *Saffron*, like other early San Juan boats, had a plywood pad between the upper deck and the lining of the inside ceiling. Upon this was mounted the mast, which in turn was supported for only half of its width by a teak two-by-four. This left the starboard side of the mast literally sitting on two thin layers of fibreglass and a piece of plywood. The wires that led to the top of the mast went through the deck and wood. On a new boat this likely was all right, but my boat was over five years old and had endured Vancouver rains plus fearful strain in that violent gale.

I did not notice that the top deck began to develop a hollow on one side of the mast. I did not like to ask the two local San Juan skippers for advice because we were in hot competition, but I did find out later that Seattle owners had long since doubled up on the compression post that supported the mast, sometimes to the extent of taking a steel tube right down to the keel. They had also replaced the plywood pad with more solid material.

My boat slowly deteriorated as water seeped into the rotting plywood. We did well in some races, but others were most disappointing as we were not able to point as well into the wind on one tack as our competition. We kept on trying and kept on learning. Races came and went, and today they all blur in my memory.

One race that we entered does stand out. Over the years of racing both my San Juan 24 and the C&C 25 that replaced it, we usually participated in the large Southern Straits event that is held on Easter weekend. Since this occurs right in the middle of the spring equinox, the weather varies from mostly awful to almost pleasant. One year when we entered with *Saffron*, the weather was mild. We started out off the West Vancouver shore. That year the shorter race for small boats went over to Entrance Island near Nanaimo, down to the mouth of the Fraser River, up to Halibut Banks near Sechelt, and back to Point Atkinson. Pointing well was not such a challenge on a race that comprised many runs downwind and reaches across the wind. In the middle of a long, gentle spinnaker run in moonlight from the Fraser River north, we were among a fleet of boats ghosting along in what was a slowly dying wind. Out of the dark from the direction of Howe Sound came the lights of a tug under tow. Behind it loomed two heavily loaded barges.

In this case sailboats had to defer to a working boat incapable of manoeuvring. The barges would have run right up over the stern of the tug and sunk it had it attempted to stop. The skipper began frantically sounding his horn as some boats relentlessly moved into the path of danger. Finally we all doused our sails except for one ignorant or stubborn owner who refused to give way. In desperation, the tugboat cast free its burden and scrambled around behind the barges in an attempt to pick up the trailing line that drags astern. In the dark and the shouting we could not see what happened, but it appeared that the sailboat went blissfully on its way, leaving the tugboat skipper to make sense out of his tangled mess. Needless to say, the race committee heard about that infraction. And since the wind was almost non-existent, we were all stopped in our tracks for a while. We finished well down the pack.

Through all my racing, no matter how awful the weather, Michelle James was with me. Aside from doing most of the foredeck work, she organized the crew, assigned food provisioning, and timed all my racing starts. I had enough on my plate keeping the boat in shape and taking wet sails home to rinse and dry in the bathtub, all the while commuting the 40 miles from Abbotsford. We entered every race available for the ten years we were together as a female team.

I made sure that Michelle became experienced helming the boat so that I could get some relief on longer races. This was one of the best decisions I ever made because in one race, which began near the Point Grey bell buoy, we bobbed around in light air while the larger boats began their starts. Then a sudden blast of wind hit us before our gun went off. Michelle hurriedly put on a smaller headsail and we took off. As we tensioned the boom-vang, its block disintegrated, so I handed her the tiller and dashed below for a spare. While all this was going on, two tugs hauling booms into the Fraser had entered the start area. She had to steer through a narrow slot between them, using only the power of the genoa as the main was out of commission.

As a pair, we became quite skilled and aggressive at the start line, earning respect from other skippers, and we gradually accumulated awards for being among the top three boats to finish.

I had no idea when I began that racing would become addictive, but it did. And the outcome exceeded my wildest dreams. I felt that I was master of the universe. I could sail that boat anywhere!

Expanding Horizons

Although I spent winters racing, I still travelled to Desolation Sound for the summer months, the habit too strong to break. Alan joined me for the first two holidays and would have kept coming if I had thought to bring along a buddy for him. But he had enough of cruising with just mom by the third year, so elected to stay home and run the household with his older brother. With my wonderful in-laws right next door and our neighbours, the Dunkerleys, on the other side, this was not a foolish move on my part. (Mrs. Dunkerley had been their babysitter for years.) Also, I felt that my sons needed to learn to stand on their own two feet.

I will never forget my first solo trip to Cortes Island. The sunny weather and gentle southeast wind made it a spinnaker run. It was hot as I ghosted up past Texada Island, so I took off all my clothes. Because tanning in the early 1980s was not yet thought of as a thing to be avoided, I started erasing some of the areas of white. Now and then I doused myself with a bucket of salt water to cool off. The ocean chuckled as it passed around the hull, and in answer, the tiller quivered under my hand. The boat and I had become extensions of each other and I was completely oblivious to anything except our immediate path and the billowing of the gorgeous spinnaker until the roar of a plane passing close overhead woke me to the presence of the surrounding world.

Then I noticed that I was overtaking two large, heavy sailboats. To my surprise, one of these turned out to be the ketch that I had been involved in building for all those years in my backyard in Abbotsford before I, as a wife, was traded in for a younger model. I slipped on a shirt, gave them lots of room, and headed forward into the beautiful day. Some of the healing had begun. It does take a long time to undo the damage, but getting involved in racing was helping me to recover my self-esteem.

I was often joined in my summer travels by crew members such as Eleanor Frisk, Sharleen Griffin, and Michelle James, who came to share the joys of salmon

Michelle James proudly displays a perch she caught off the Cortes Bay dock. Michelle went on to become an economist for Fisheries and Oceans.

fishing, sailing, and exploring beaches. We put in many harbour days where they learned how to catch the elusive perch that hid under the wharves. My daughter also came each year from Princeton, New Jersey, where her scholarships had led her into doctoral studies in economics.

Frequently I anchored in Smelt Bay, revelled in Nellie Jeffery's hospitality, and also took her for sailing outings. Like me, Nellie had almost been born with a pair of oars in her hands. She took to sailing with great ease. We were both intrigued by Native rock art, so went searching out examples whenever we could.

One summer, Eleanor Frisk and I got up the courage to traverse the Yuculta Rapids, one of the three possible routes to northern waters. I found John Chappell's book *Cruising Beyond Desolation Sound* a wonderful guide, as there was little other help at the time. I bought nearly all the charts that he recommended (they were cheap then), and we followed his route, finally ending up at Minstrel Island in Knight Inlet. The old hotel was still standing, clinging to the steep edge of a small island. It had the appearance of a place that would eventually collapse from sheer fatigue as a result of the heavy use given it by loggers and fishermen in earlier days (instead it burned down the following winter). Liquor laws in B.C. were kind to hoteliers because beer parlours, which were restricted to hotels, were often the only sources of alcohol for thirsty folk. On weekends these places were really busy. As for us, we explored and ate well, catching salmon or crab whenever we felt the need, as this whole area was a sports-fishing mecca.

In those days, young Native people had not yet realized what a gold mine they had in their heritage, which made it possible for us to inspect the ancient settlement of Mamalilaculla at our leisure. The gently sloping beach, white with discarded clam shells, was crowned with berry bushes. These seem to thrive in the nutritious soil of the old settlements. Above the beach and mounted on stilts were one-roomed cabins that I assumed were for the storage and mending of gillnets. But since there were bits of furniture and old mattress springs inside, they might well have been pressed into service as dwellings.

Behind these there were a number of Art Deco houses, all grey and denuded of paint, with broken window glass and blackberry vines creeping through the openings. Beside one, we almost stumbled over two sea creatures carved of wood and lying parallel in the deep grass. They looked rather like alligators with their gaping jaws studded with teeth. Behind the same building, peering out from under the branch of a scrubby apple tree, we found a totem pole bearing an aristocratic Native head crowning the head of a bear. This pole leaned sadly toward the house, and when I saw it again a few years later it was lying on its back with rain water puddled in the hollows.

This totem (left) had the most hauntingly beautiful human figure atop a bear head. It was lying in the weeds the second time I visited Mamalilaculla, while the pole at right fell a few years later.

One of a pair of longhouse roof supports at Mamalilaculla. These massive logs are more than 30 inches in diameter and intricately adzed.

Just to the left, beside another old home, were two massive house support posts that bore a third post across their tops, nestled in matching hollows to keep it secure. These 30-inch-diameter cedar logs had been smoothed, then decorated by bands of adze marks. For about two feet these adze grooves went around the pole. Then there was a section where they were perpendicular; then the rings recurred. The effect was decidedly Grecian. A matching set of posts at the far end of the clearing indicated the original size of this impressive longhouse.

As we pushed our way through tangled bushes, we could see a totem that rose up over the top of all the trees. A sort of trail had been cleared to the base, but because it was surrounded by growth on all sides we could not photograph its full glory, only stare in awe. A few years later, this pole also tumbled down, with the top projecting out over the beach.

The atmosphere of the place so haunted me that I returned many times, watching the deterioration of those poles and of the net storage houses that perched above the shore. One year, after the tallest pole lost its killer whale to the sea, I spoke to the young man who seemed to be summer custodian. He said that they made no attempt to preserve their art because all things eventually decay and the whale was simply returning to its home.

In my own heart I somehow forgave those who took pieces of this magnificent art form to museums. Had they not done so there would be few examples available for the young Native artists of today as they attempt to rebuild their heritage. This village had remained occupied longer than many because the children had not been removed to be put into residential schools. These schools, accompanied by our gifts of disease and alcohol, had gone a long way toward destroying an entire culture.

As the days shortened for us that first summer up north, I reluctantly pointed the nose of the boat toward Cortes, but Knight Inlet would see me again. After Eleanor headed home, Michelle James hitched a ride upcoast so she could help with the hundred-mile run to Vancouver. She arrived with her arm in a cast from a soccer injury. One-armed or not, I was glad to see her.

Squitty Bay on a peaceful summer day.

We stopped at Westview, near Powell River, for provisions. Since neither of us had explored the far side of Texada Island, we decided to try that route. A lively southeaster kept us busy tacking our way along the shore of that long island, finally urging us into Scotty Bay at the northwest end of Lasqueti Island. This turned out to be a fortuitous choice of anchorage because that night the wind blew 72 knots. The rigging screamed. We were not alone in that secure cove. It was crowded, but the only boats that shifted were two small cruisers that had rafted up on one anchor. The bottom was mud, glorious mud. This is the bay of choice to ride out a southeaster.

The storm continued to rage through the next day, so I rowed my dinghy through the waves to a beach on the outer island to dig clams. Fighting the slop, where my oars took on a life of their own, reminded me of my youthful days spent rowboat fishing the waters of Cortes Island. The struggle became a joy. The clam feast wasn't hard to take either.

The next day we tried for home but ended up at the south end of Lasqueti Island in Squitty Bay, finding partial shelter from the residue of the storm. It was the long weekend before school started, so we had to leave next morning. We decided to try for Secret Cove, where we could tie up the boat and catch the bus to Vancouver. We ventured out into the mess. However, when we aimed across the passage toward our goal, we found that the wind and waves were totally out of sync. On one tack we were in the trough and did well. On the other tack we were heading right into the waves, which stopped us dead in the water. We finally gave up and headed back upcoast to Pender Harbour, which was crowded with others in the same fix. The bus next morning was loaded with people talking about lost dinghies and gear that had broken loose and drifted away while they struggled homeward. It had become an insurance adjuster's nightmare.

On that trip I met Paul Holsinger, who regularly summered with friends near Cortes Bay. He, too, was a teacher and sailed a pretty 26-foot Hereshoff-style wooden boat. In time, with so many common interests, we became good buddies. Next summer I left *Saffron* in Vancouver for my crew to use, and Paul and I began cruising farther north in his boat. He was a fantastically gifted machinist and I, by that time, was a knowledgeable sailor, so we made a good team. We travelled together for three summers, eventually feeling brave enough to make the crossing to the Queen Charlotte Islands (though this is a story for another book).

Michelle made good use of my boat. She had become skilled in all aspects of boat handling, so she holidayed on it with her future husband, Wally Raepple. They named their young golden retriever after the boat, and I'm sure both Saffrons enjoyed their summers.

One year the crew decided to enter the Maple Bay regatta near Sidney on Vancouver Island. I had never done this race because by the time it was held, I was always off upcoast. At the start line they were in a nasty collision with another boat, putting a decided damper on their fun and a damaged bow on my boat. Doing the starts (where your neck is always swivelling while you avoid other boats) had been my responsibility, with Michelle on the stopwatch, so it was partly my fault as this was one area of their training that I had neglected.

The upshot of all this was that I decided in the fall of 1983 that it was time to get a boat in which I did not have to kneel to cook or to do the dishes. Paul's boat, *Wood Duck*, and mine both lacked headroom. By that time I had figured out why *Saffron*'s mast would not stay tuned, so I removed it, had the deck reinforced, and doubled up the teak support post. The crew had already had the bow repaired, so except for a slight discrepancy in colour, the boat looked good.

My new boat was a C&C 25, *Papillion*, which coincidentally had protested me years earlier when I was a novice sailor. This sleek but sturdy craft was produced in Ontario at the C&C yard and was an instant success. It was considered by many to be the Mercedes Benz of small sailboats and remained popular long after the company ceased to exist. Built in 1973, *Papillion* was a year older than *Saffron* but many pounds heavier, and it also allowed me to stand in the area of the galley. It took me another year to sell *Saffron*, but I didn't care— my back was truly happy.

A few weeks after I had purchased the new boat, Michelle asked if I could come into town on a Wednesday evening so we could talk over some of the things that needed attention. She met me in the parking lot and we proceeded to the boat. The hull seemed a bit low in the water, but I figured that I was unfamiliar with how it should look. Imagine my surprise when I removed the door boards and found the vessel crammed with balloons, champagne, and all the women who had become part of my crew. It was a boat-warming party, but the warmest thing was our hearts. My eyes brimmed with tears. Together we decided that the boat's new name should be *Juno*, the powerful queen of the gods, as *Papillion* seemed a bit too flighty.

The first task was to remove the mast and re-rig it because it was not geared for racing. I set to work redesigning the sail-handling gear so that all the colour-keyed lines, even those for reefing the mainsail, would lead to the cockpit. Wally took the mast home and added ports into which lines disappeared at the top, only to reappear near the base. We added a plate on top with a pair of halyard blocks. Never again would I race with only one available halyard. We added new winches and sheet-stoppers so that all heavy jobs could be handled by winches when necessary. Since I knew I would be travelling farther north, often alone, I wanted a rig that was safe and easy to handle. And that's what I got.

The boat was a delight to race. Downwind under spinnaker was like driving a truck. There was no unsteadiness or broaches where the ocean tried to climb into the cockpit. During one night-run in the heavier boat from Entrance Island all the way to the channel marker near the mouth of the Fraser River, we roared along in the dark on large waves. Now and then the hull would fit nicely onto the leading side of the wave and hold there with the knot meter rising to ten (it could go no further), sticking there during the exhilarating surge forward, which ended with the boat settling into the foam that boiled up on either side as the crest of the wave passed underneath. This happened over and over again, filling my heart with great joy.

Juno needed heavier air to get moving, so I had Gerry Storch build a light sail called a drifter. This particular one was no larger than half a bedsheet. If we found ourselves in a spot with no wind but the inevitable confusion of boat wakes, this bit of spinnaker cloth would tweak the boat along in tiny pulls so that we could work our way over to where the breeze was marking the ocean with ghostly streaks.

By this time our sail inventory was impressive, expanded as it was by a couple of dandies from my friend Al Crowe when he sold his C&C 25 and moved on to a bigger boat to fit his growing family. The best hand-me-over was the flat, heavy-duty spinnaker that helped keep the boat on its feet if the wind piped up or came more abeam. For beating to weather in strong winds I no longer was stuck with the little storm jib. Now I had a sturdy blade sail that maintained its shape and kept us moving, even in the worst conditions.

We raced this boat with glee. In little air we could not compete with ultra-light boats, but our knowledge had increased to the point that it often compensated for lack of speed. When the wind blew we were competitive, soon adding to our stock of trophies. I had long since begun sharing these with the regular crew as I was running out of wall space. Bay races became our delight. By then we were getting the hang of currents and quick sail changes. We enjoyed mark roundings, where you make a sudden change to spinnaker after beating to weather. On a downwind run we often used spinnaker jibes to catch the best angle of air. And we delighted in trying to peel the paint off the transom of another boat as we crossed behind it while we were on a port tack. We frequently took honours of the year for boats of our size.

Participating in what were sometimes wet and miserable overnight races was much easier on *Juno* because she had leeboards to keep you in the bunk when the boat heaved around, and a kerosene furnace to keep you warm. The usual way to light the furnace involved filling a small cup under the burner with alcohol. You lit this to pre-heat the element because kerosene has a high flashpoint and smokes repulsively if you try to ignite it cold. It was impossible and dangerous to fill this cup when we were underway, so I'd use a propane torch and play it around on the metal base of the burner to the count of 90 seconds before turning on the fuel supply. This sounds like a dangerous procedure, but I braced myself well, got it going, and the crew members gratefully took turns below in the bunk to thaw out.

One invention of the time was an added blessing in our efforts to avoid hypothermia. Fabric manufacturers produced a synthetic fleece that did not absorb water. I bought an outfit of this material to wear under my rain gear, and it made life bearable. It covered my body snugly from ankle to armpit, with zippers on the outside of the legs. The real treasure was another zipper that went all the way from your navel, under the crotch, and up to your waist in the back. Using the toilet in freezing weather was no longer the bum-chiller that it used to be.

Sometimes my youthful days as a rowboat fisherman were a definite asset. I was not afraid of shallow water. During one Fraser River Lightship race we had to round Point Grey and cross to the north arm of the Fraser River, which has a powerful current. The wind was coming from the same direction as the flow of the river. We rounded the point and slipped in close to Wreck Beach (famed for its nude bathers). *Juno*'s depth sounder was awkwardly placed inside the cabin, so I had a crew member below calling out the depths. We were there to stay out of the opposing current and use the back-eddy, but sometimes we barely cleared the ocean bottom.

We reset the spinnaker and surged out of the mouth of the north arm of the river with the current helping us along. We joined in with the larger boats that were approaching on our right and carried on toward the south arm, where we rounded the marker and headed back to the finish line. We came in first in our class in elapsed time and first in corrected time, which didn't hurt my feelings at all.

We were able to use this tactic again the next year in the Southern Straits competition. Prior to that race I had driven all the way from Abbotsford to West Vancouver Yacht Club to attend a seminar at which our arch rival was one of the featured speakers. He was supposed to give us tips on how to win this difficult race, but he firmly declared that he wasn't about to reveal any of his trade secrets for crossing the mouth of the river, in spite of a chiding from the chairman. To my great satisfaction we went on to beat him in corrected time, although we were well down the pack behind two larger boats, two fast Martin 242s, a C&C 26, and *Nebo*, a Ranger 33.

I no longer did the single-handed race because the headsails had to be fed into a track or slot when raised, and hauled down by hand when lowered, but for me, the reason for doing that race no longer existed. I knew that I could sail alone, especially when I substituted a roller-furling headsail in the summertime. Now, with a simple pull on a line, the genoa would roll up like a window blind. I eventually purchased an automatic pilot and a canvas dodger to deflect the wind and rain, which made single-handing a pleasure.

As a crew we did three more Juan de Fuca races in *Juno*, bringing my total to six in all. The first of these races in the bigger boat found us struggling around in dense fog. With four other lives my responsibility, the problem of not knowing exactly where I was made me decide then and there that a Loran navigation device was imperative. The global positioning system was not yet available, and Loran still cost upwards of $1,400, but I vowed never to let myself

Juno's racing crew before a Juan de Fuca race out of Victoria, left to right, Wendy Grider, Carol Cardew, June, Rosemary Anderson, and Michelle James.

feel so lost in the fog again. We put it to immediate use in various middle-distance races, and it repaid us instantly with a great boost in confidence.

I returned early from one race in June and decided to surprise the current love of my life with an unexpected visit. What was really unexpected was the collection of cocktail napkins on his kitchen table with the names and phone numbers of various cuties. I was overcome with the need to run away to sea.

Eleanor was between jobs and up for adventure, so we elected to take the boat out Juan de Fuca Strait as far as Barkley Sound. Once there, I ran out of both charts and steam. After a short holiday around the area, Eleanor took the bus home and I hung around the fishing village of Ucluelet, where my brother had lived as a fisherman until

*Eleanor Frisk in the mouth of a cave near the abandoned
Native village on Effingham Island in Barkley Sound.*

his early death at 49, and where my mother's sister Nora still lived
with her second husband, Jack Biggin-Pound. Not only had Jack
trained at a major British art school, but he was also an outstanding
photographer. I had a darkroom and was eager to learn what I could
about camera work, so we spent hours out taking pictures. And since
Nora's voice echoed my mother's, I revelled in their hospitality.

My son Al came out by car with his future wife, Deb Williams.
The fishing was outstanding. Deb was determined to learn how to
gut fish, and she got lots of practice as the largest catch was a
24-pound spring salmon. Both Deb and I were underwhelmed by
my minuscule rubber dinghy. It had come with the boat and was
basically a child's toy. But we managed, by dint of relays, to all get
ashore on Effingham Island so that we could examine the sea caves
and the glorious old Native village site. Deb proved to all of us that
she could fit into our nautical lifestyle. They drove back to

Abbotsford loaded with fish and adventures to talk about for years to come.

In late summer Eleanor returned and we began the trip home. The Loran had driven me to distraction because whenever I shut it down it lost all its memory. We had to spend time every morning entering the latitude and longitude of waypoints, whereas usually these co-ordinates remain in memory. Once the waypoints were installed I could ask the device to guide me where I wanted to go, to tell me if I got off course, to give me my speed over the bottom of the ocean (a rather important bit of information in the big currents of the straits), and to alert me when I reached my destination. It is easy to see why I wanted this tool for navigating this often foggy passageway.

With the two of us on board, the trip went easily. No fog, either. Certainly we were familiar with these waters, having already done six Juan de Fuca races. Nevertheless it is a long journey for a boat travelling no more than five knots. There is only one moderately safe harbour at nearly the halfway point, so we set out from Barkley Sound early one morning, travelled the 40 nautical miles to Port Renfrew, put in a rolly night, and did the 54-mile jaunt to Victoria the next day. The last stop was the fine harbour at Sidney. All that remained was the 40-mile stretch across the Strait of Georgia to my mooring in False Creek.

When we reached Vancouver the marine electronics store down by Coal Harbour told me that my Loran unit needed a small battery to retain its memory. Even with the high cost of this navigation equipment they had not seen fit to either supply a two-dollar item or to tell me that it was needed. I was a trifle irate.

The success of this trip opened up visions of great possibilities for me. I would look for people who wanted to join me in travelling as far north as we cared to go. Oh, the joy that comes with this discovery!

Circumnavigation Time

My life began to undergo profound changes. I knew I would have to take early retirement from teaching because of my increasing deafness. The pension would be minimal since I had spent many years at home raising both a family and vegetables while working on my undergraduate degree. Upon returning to teaching as a special education teacher, I had only worked mornings (while the marriage lasted) so that I could be home when the children returned from school. This sort of behaviour did not earn you big money upon retirement.

I knew that I had to find a way to supplement my income. A workshop for teachers at the Hotel Vancouver, in which the instructor guided us to inner revelation, had encouraged me to return to a childhood pleasure. I began to study art again. This became a joyful obsession. Back in Abbotsford, where I worked, there was an outstanding instructor who was also an accomplished portraitist. Gladys Murray opened my eyes and guided my hand as I struggled through self-doubt and began to grow as an artist.

Summer holidays on *Juno* became a time to do watercolours of boats, as that was the field I understood best. I spent many hours around Cortes Bay doing portraits of boats that caught my eye. The

I work on a watercolour while tied to Cortes Bay float. Note the weird sunshade.

graceful lines of older sailboats and traditional fishing boats became my favourites.

By this time, my children had grown and left home. My aged father invited himself to come and live with me. He had no one else, as my mother and brother were both dead. I sold the family home because I could no longer cope with three acres and a tired house, let alone an 80-year-old dad. At first we lived in an Abbotsford condominium, where he undertook to type all my essays as I worked my way through a Master of Education degree from Western Washington University in Bellingham. This institution, a pleasant half-hour drive away, had attracted a fine staff. I continued racing my boat out of Vancouver, studying art, and teaching. Condominium life was the only solution to my hectic lifestyle.

In 1985, two strokes left my dad unable to handle walking the busy streets of Abbotsford. He had to give up shopping and doing much of the cooking. He was also left without the ability to read or write, a tragedy for a writer and self-trained artist.

I decided that the easiest way out of my dilemma was to move the household to False Creek, near my boat. We bought a small ground-floor condominium in a row house overlooking a park and duck pond. There Dad began the slow process of relearning how to cook and shop. He only had to walk along the seawall to the market at Leg-in-Boot Square. The kindly owner would even deliver groceries if Dad felt particularly frail. I undertook the early morning commute 45 miles to Abbotsford. As I was going the opposite way to the heavy traffic, there were no delays. In time, my musician son Ian moved in with us, so summer holidays on *Juno* were possible as there was someone at home to help my father.

I began taking advantage of all the opportunities offered by a big city, enrolling in art classes. I made friends, some of whom even joined me for short boating holidays. By this time I had learned that women made better guests than men on the boat, because they always did more than their share of the chores.

In 1987, retirement became a fact. I felt that, because of deafness, I was no longer meeting the needs of the children entrusted to my care. One of my racing crew members, Diane Fast, had finished her residency in psychiatry and was ready for a break before commencing what would become a busy practice. Diane and I had long since made up our minds that a circumnavigation of Vancouver Island would be a suitable reward at this time in our lives, and we started making plans for this trip.

My father, now 89, had been in the process of dying all that spring, but was hanging on as long as he could. He had been expected to die much earlier in the year because his weight was down to 80 pounds and he had virtually stopped eating. He was at the stage of diapers and a wheelchair, with nursing provided by Ian, an afternoon care worker, and me. We kept him at home because it made him happy, but as the summer holidays approached, and with the help and encouragement of our much-loved family physician Elaine Wynne, I reluctantly put Dad in the Brock Fahrni building at Shaughnessy Hospital where, as a First World War veteran, he was most welcome. Next morning Diane and I set out on our trip.

I spent the first afternoon patching the trailing edge of our mainsail, as I had discovered in the rush that I had only brought the old spare. This was likely just as well, because it would spend most of the upcoming two months exposed to the sun. It had become my habit to motor along with the main raised but tied down firmly amidships, as this minimized rolling in any sort of a swell.

The two lads we rescued as they were being pushed rapidly upcoast near Westview in 1987.

Besides giving a more comfortable ride, this arrangement meant we were ready should the wind pipe up. The second afternoon found us approaching Westview Harbour, sailing ahead of a fairly brisk southeast wind. Imagine our surprise when we came upon two young boys vigorously paddling an inflatable toy dinghy upwind in the direction of Grief Point. They were losing ground steadily and looked ready to burst into tears.

We quickly doused our sails, went back, and loaded them onboard. Apparently they had been playing near the beach at Grief Point and had been swept away in the wind. They hadn't realized that cutting diagonally into the shore downwind and carrying the craft home would have been the ideal solution. At the dock we passed them into the grateful arms of their uncle, a member of the local coast guard crew. He thanked us profusely and said he felt it had been a lesson well learned. The mother's only comment when we spoke to her on the phone was, "Oh. I wondered where they were."

That evening I phoned Alan and he said he had just returned from attending the death of my father that afternoon. At this I burst into tears. Diane, capable psychiatrist that she was, said it had been a fair exchange—the life of two little boys for the life of one old man. When I eventually told this story to my Cortes Island friend Nellie, she quietly observed that perhaps my father had been guiding our path. And perhaps he had.

Diane and I meandered lazily up the remaining 200 miles of the inside coast of Vancouver Island. I shared with her all my favourite haunts, including Mamalilaculla. We stopped at Port Hardy, the last available supply depot, to top up our fuel and water tanks and get fresh groceries. In order to reach the west coast we had to deal with one last navigational hazard ... the Nahwitti Bar, named for the Nahwitti tribe that had peopled this coastline when Europeans first reached these waters.

The tip of Vancouver Island is composed largely of sand, with rocky outcroppings to give it form. A chain of islands skirting its mainland side ends with one named Hope. Over the years, the current that surges around the top of Vancouver Island has built up an impressive underwater bar between the shore and Hope Island. Here, the ocean floor goes from a depth of 30 feet to almost 200 feet over the distance of about a city block.

Diane and I had timed our arrival at Bull Harbour on Hope Island so that we could leave there and cross the Nahwitti Bar at slack tide in the early morning. This was the ideal because afternoon northwesterlies would make rounding Cape Scott unpleasant. On our approach to Bull Harbour from Port Hardy we had a chance to observe the action at the bar. While a big current swept us along toward the bar, it was being battered by a strong northwest wind coming from the opposite direction. The combers were gigantic, a towering wall of breaking seas. We gladly left this awesome sight and turned in to shelter.

At Bull Harbour our luck ran out. A series of violent storms kept us and many cruisers and fishing boats locked up in that secure place for three days. Each day moved the timing of the bar crossing an hour later. In boredom and frustration we finally rowed over to visit a nearby fishing boat. I wanted to ask the fisherman if he had known my brother, George Griffin, while he was alive and fishing these waters.

For years my brother had begged me to leave my kids with my husband for part of the summer and join him as crew so he could share with me the glory and beauty of the coast that he loved. My sense of duty held me back, and after his early death I often regretted my choice. I had determined that on this trip I would visit as many of his favourite anchorages as I could, to see if I could find him again.

The fisherman had not known George. Conversation veered around to the weather. I grumbled that the hour of slack tide for crossing the bar was getting later and later each day. He looked at me in amazement and asked, "Lady, why would you want to cross the bar?"

I replied, "How else will I reach Cape Scott?"

Out came a chart and three bottles of beer. He showed us two possible routes for bypassing the hazard. If you were heading from Bull Harbour to Rivers Inlet on the mainland side, you worked your way along the coast of Hope Island, through the various breakers (hidden rocks over which ocean swells break), until you were past the shallow area and then you turned northeast toward the B.C. coast. But if you were heading for Cape Scott you merely crossed to the Vancouver Island shore and worked along near the sandy beach in about eighteen feet of water, keeping the kelp beds of Tatnall Reef between you and the bar until you were clear.

Next morning found us happily on our way, skirting the Vancouver Island shore. The breeze picked up early that day. Before long we had the sails set and were slogging the three-hour beat out to the Cape. Fortunately the current was in our favour. We kept well offshore because the fisherman had warned us to stay clear of the Cape to avoid the turbulence that develops near the point. The waters were too lively that day for a dinghy visit to the old Cape Scott settlement, so we reluctantly passed by. However, the fisherman had also told us that the harbour between Cox and its neighbouring island on our right was a

*We round Cape Scott with a real
growler of a wave mounting astern.*

treasure trove of Japanese flotsam. I already had a collection of glass fishing-net balls, shampoo bottles, and the like that had made the trans-Pacific journey, but I wanted Diane to experience the thrill of discovery.

We could see a huge log carrier high up on the shore of Cox Island. It had broken loose from its tug in a south-east gale a few years earlier and piled up on the beach with its precious load of timber. Since the wind was from the northwest we reasoned that there would be shelter in the lee of the islands, but as we headed in to shore we were hit by a blast of air that shook the rigging and literally tore the wind indicator off the top of the mast. A powerful venturi funnelled the wind between the hills, tripling its force. At that point the roller furling wouldn't furl, so I had to crawl forward with a screwdriver and free the jammed line. I thanked the sea gods for providing me with a capable deck hand. Diane had raced with me in many conditions of weather and knew exactly what to do.

By this time the winds had built into a fury, so we sailed down the outer coast of Vancouver Island, went by the entrance to Sea Otter Cove as it looked hazardous in those conditions, and tucked gratefully into a niche on the north side of nearby San Josef Bay. We launched our dinghy, stretched our legs on the sandy beach, saw our first evidence of sea kayakers, set the crab trap, and settled in for a quiet night. It was. Next morning we found in the trap the biggest Dungeness crab that I had ever seen, so our visit brought supper as well as the satisfaction of having rounded the Cape.

*Well-pounded sand surrounds rocky outcroppings in San Josef Bay
where Cape Scott settlers struggled to maintain a dock.*

Cape Scott II, *in San Josef Bay, c.1916. Settler and mariner, Captain Henry
Peterson in command with Nora Peterson on deck, while they approach the dock in
the San Josef River. Bow of rowboat used for fording the river can be seen.*

An old-time fisherman later warned us that a wind shift to the southeast would have put us in big trouble. We would have become fully exposed to the wind and (lacking radar) not been able to work off the lee shore in the dark, let alone find the opposite side of the bay.

San Josef Bay offered precarious shelter years earlier when the Danish settlement at Cape Scott tried to find an all-weather port for freight boats. These hardy people established farms at the Cape in 1896 after the Minister of Immigration at Victoria signed an agreement that a road would be built from the colony to San Josef Bay. The road never appeared. The nearest port available to the farms was at Fishermans Bay, which supported no permanent landing because it was wide open to northwesterly storms. Cattle could be made to swim ashore, but there was no way to reverse the process so that they could be loaded for shipment to market.

In later years pioneers built a wharf up the river at San Josef Bay. One of the settlers, Captain Henry Peterson, managed to worm the freight boat *Cape Scott* up to this dock at high tide by surging in with the swell, dodging two great rocks, and bumping his way over sunken logs. But there was still no road, so everything coming or going to the farms had to either walk or be backpacked. And with no way to get their produce to market, these hardy souls eventually deserted the whole area of the Cape. It is now a park, with land access still limited to footpaths.

Had I had the time to re-read the account of the Cape Scott venture before we left for the trip around Vancouver Island, I would have searched the area upstream of the San Josef River mouth and found the huge stone that marks the grave of Captain Peterson, who was buried near the landing on the riverbank. His son Lester was a special friend of mine. He wrote *The Cape Scott Story* and also the history of the Sechelt Nation before his untimely death from multiple sclerosis.

As it was, we simply absorbed the beauty, spent the next night in Sea Otter Cove, where we followed the ribbon-marked trail to the outer beach, then up-anchored and moved down the coast to Winter Harbour. There we took on gas (more about that later). The fuel

Juno at Winter Harbour float. Diane resorted to jogging back and forth on the dock after disturbing a mother bear with cubs when she tried running on the gravel road out of town.

depot, a fish-buying barge, a small store, and a few scattered houses were all that remained of a once-active community, and there was no sign of the cannery that specialized in clam and crab, providing work for local people. Before the turn of the century there had been a large Native population that had welcomed a group of Norwegian settlers with gifts of fish. Now there was only a small reserve nearby, but a kindly old Native man on a fishboat gave us a salmon fillet for our dinner, so the tradition remains.

With the help of a fellow sailor, I was able to fix the roller-furling drum. When I had reassembled it that spring I had left too much clearance between the drum and the housing. The thin line could jump into this gap and leave me unable to furl the sail. What would have been a nuisance during inner-coast sailing could be a disaster out here.

Diane was pleased to find that Winter Harbour's road gave her a chance to stretch her legs with an early morning run. However, she returned rather abruptly and somewhat out of breath to say she had

Sea lions at Solander Island protesting our arrival.

surprised a mother bear and two cubs along the way. She solved her dilemma by running back and forth on the government dock instead.

That evening we met two young commercial fishermen on a rather primitive troller called *Allons* (French for "Let's go"). These brothers not only gave us information about safe good anchorages, but also told us to give them a call on channel seven before we set out to round the cape at Solander Island. They said they'd rather stop what they were doing to answer our call than try to rescue us if anything went wrong. (With all the help, advice, and free salmon, I thought myself a pretty smart skipper to have brought along such a beautiful deck hand.)

A few days later, after overnighting at Klaskino Anchorage down the coast and after a successful early morning of salmon trolling near Lawn Point, we called *Allons* on channel seven. One of the brothers answered our query and said, "Come on. It's a pussycat out here." And, truly, it was. The ocean showed not a ripple on top of the long smooth Pacific swells. Solander Island and Cape Cook have a justified reputation of knowing the worst winds on the outer coast of Vancouver Island, but not that day.

So we cleaned and stored our catch, fired up the nine-horse-power Honda outboard, and set out to round the halfway mark of our voyage. To our delight, chunky black-and-white puffins with their distinctive orange beaks buzzed by wearing ragged moustaches of herring as they hurried to their nests on the grassy inner slope of Solander Island. Sea lions moaned as we neared the shore, and the swells covered and uncovered the smooth lower shores of this wind-and-wave-sculpted rock.

Typical mooring buoys maintained by the fisheries department for commercial fishing boats in harbours with dubious holding ground. These buoys were usually held in place by cables that stretched crisscross on the seabed.

Except for the few salmon trollers and a lone kayaker out on the water, the area seemed empty, yet I found out much later from my friend Joe Christensen that tiny cabins had been left standing here and there along the shore for victims of shipwrecks. As a young man, he prospected most of the peninsula of Cape Cook, at first by helicopter and later, with another gold seeker, by runabout boat. They panned their way from stream to stream all the way from Gold River to Solander, and now and then they stumbled on one of these isolated, primitive shelters.

He also found a shack, leftover lumber, and evidence that a boat had been built at Canoe Landing, which is on an Indian reserve at the southwest corner of the Cape. When he asked about this anomaly at Kyuquot, he learned that a white South African by the name of Neaves had lived at this godforsaken spot years earlier while he struggled to create a fishing boat by hand out of local and beachcombed lumber. He was almost done when he died. Joe said that although the boat was gone, daffodils still bloomed here and there amid the wild splendour.

As we travelled down the outer coast of Vancouver Island we tried out nearly every anchorage, sometimes tying to one of the many mooring buoys placed in bays where anchoring was not practical. These tie-ups are usually secured by long underwater cables that go from shore to shore, so boaters must take care not to foul these if they do have to drop the hook. I found that the metal caps on these buoys scarred my fibreglass bow when we rode up on them as the tide changed, so I contrived a bib of fenders to protect the finish. That year I had bought a rubber inflatable that just fitted the foredeck. I also had a two-horse outboard which allowed us to leave the large boat in a secure place and ride the tender to outlying spots.

In the ship's library we had a book entitled *Edible? Incredible!* and we sampled all the sea had to offer. Stripping the white muscle from inside a sea cucumber could only be done after a large gin and tonic, as it was a nauseating process. The sea cucumber disgorges its intestines the minute it feels pain, and we almost did the same. But when I sautéed the bits in oil and butter they had a delicate abalone flavour without the toughness. We finally drew the line at gumboot chitons. They are correctly named and there was no way we could make the foot chewable.

On trips ashore we would refer to another book, *Northwestern Wild Berries*, which had us tasting regularly, often making wry faces at the result of our choices. The author would comment that such-and-such a berry was edible, adding the note "Who'd want to?" and we hastened to agree.

Sometimes we hiked along primitive trails to outer beaches in the fond hope that we would find the treasured glass balls. These balls escape from fishing nets along the coast of Japan and can take up to seven years to reach the B.C. coast. More often than not we found evidence of kayakers, with their many footprints marking the sand. When there were no telltale bits of surveyors ribbon to mark the trail, we took to looking back at where we had come from so as to imprint the return paths in our memory.

Friends had told Diane that there was a Native dugout hidden on an island in Battle Bay, so we put in a day there searching all the knolls. We never thought to check out the island right in front of the old village site, but we did venture into a narrow slit in the cliffs to the right of the village. Timing the swells, we climbed onto a bladderwrack-shrouded rock, slid the inflatable over this obstruction, then, pushed along by the next surge, paddled the short distance to the beach.

This totem at Battle Bay was part of a house roof support.

We stepped out onto rolly pebbles and found ourselves surrounded by a rock wall, fringed with tufts of liquorice-scented ferns and dripping moss. Imagine our surprise to find a skeleton tucked under the lip of the overhanging ledge. It appeared to be a drowning victim, an ancient one, and must have been washed in here by the swells. It was not the remains of an average North American because there were no holes or fillings in the teeth. Diane said it seemed to be an adult male, so we were left with a puzzle. Nearby was a child's rubber ball with oriental cartoon figures decorating the band, an obvious visitor from across the ocean. We left it there in hopes that travellers with a child might find it. At least its discovery would help to ease the stress of finding a skeleton.

The standing totem in among the scrub growth at the village site helped us imagine earlier days when the area supported families. That night I had reason to envy those long-ago residents who could pull their boats up on the beach. I had anchored behind a long, low point of rocks in good holding ground, but during the night the wind switched to southeast. By midnight it had worked its way up to swells that were a good three feet in depth. Meanwhile, the tide had risen to cover most of the point that I had hoped would afford us shelter. I got up several times during the night and paid out every foot of anchor line, asking a few favours of the god that looked after us. I guess she listened because we woke up in the morning to find ourselves again behind the sheltering point, which had risen like a phoenix from the ashes of the night. (Oh, negligent skipper, to have forgotten to check the tide book.)

We moved a few miles downcoast through Gay Passage and explored the Bunsby Islands, spying on the resident sea otters as they rolled themselves in kelp to keep from drifting away while they took a nap. It reminded me of youthful summers as a fisherman, when I hooked a kelp-head through my oarlock as an anchor so I could rest at midday. We moved quietly, and when the otters glanced our way they simply yawned, scratched an ear, then went back to sleep. We were grateful that naturalists had transplanted these amusing creatures from Alaska to replace those that had been exterminated by the early fur-traders.

The run to Kyuquot, nine miles downcoast, took us alongside steep bluffs. Fortunately, this route is inside the protective shelter of scattered reefs called the Barrier Islands, which dampen the Pacific swells. The village of Kyuquot can only be reached by corkscrewing past numerous marked rocks that make the entryway a challenge. The Native settlement is across the bay from the fisherman's float to which we tied, but an enterprising youngster from the village was soon ensconced on our back deck. He had long since learned that he could play on the sympathy of visiting boaters, telling us how some former visitor to the site had paid to send him all the way to Expo in Vancouver. As we weren't up to a repeat of this, we fed him and his buddies what goodies we could spare before gently prying them loose from the inside of our cabin and sending them on their way.

A fog-shrouded West Coast salmon troller.

The first thing that greeted us when we ventured up the passageway called Kyuquot Sound was a totally bald island, aptly named Surprise. Every tree had been cut. It always amazes me when a logging company exhibits such a total disregard for aesthetics. We usually ignore what we cannot readily see, but it is difficult to avoid scenes that are forced upon you. Since this clearcut occurred sometime before 1987, I hope that the view of Surprise has now improved.

Rain further dampened our spirits as we motored around the inland side of Union Island in order to avoid the awesome jumble of reefs to seaward. When we could again see open water, we dropped the hook in the shelter of Rugged Point near the southern exit of Kyuquot Sound. An exploration of the outer beach revealed no glass balls, but by now Diane had taken to gathering the coloured oval foam floats that had also drifted across the Pacific. Since no one else seemed to be collecting these, she accumulated quite a few.

We hiked back toward our dinghy, pockets bulging, only to be greeted by a bedraggled party of kayakers who were hard at work unpacking their duffle. This was to be their last night of camping in what had been a damp week. Tomorrow they'd head back to their cars at Gold River. The oldest member of the party was in his eighties and had aggravated a hernia, so he and Diane went into a conference. He felt that since he'd soon be home, he'd manage. We felt a trifle guilty as we lit up our heater in the cabin to dry out while we made supper. As this did not seem too secure an overnight spot, we motored on to Catchalot Inlet, set our crab pots, and found that the bay lived up to its name.

Next morning we emerged from the inlet before the wind had built up much strength, so we unfurled the genoa, ducked around Rugged Point, and slipped along Clear Passage, inshore of large rocks awash in Pacific swells. This route also sheltered us from the turbulence that is frequently present off the mouth of large inlets, where an outgoing tide pushing water seaward can collide with opposing ocean swells. Once out into the Pacific we enjoyed a lively sail downwind all the way to the mouth of Esperanza Inlet. It was a challenge to find the buoy located far out at sea that marked the turning point through the reefs into this fascinating waterway. It seemed impossible that the marker could be so far from land, and to make matters worse, the afternoon northwesterly provided a definite beam sea when we made the turn to run in.

I think, in retrospect, the passageway behind Catala Island called the Rolling Roadstead would have been more comfortable, but I hadn't prepared myself for this the previous evening. Usually I literally memorized all the possible routes for the upcoming day, feeding the waypoints into my Loran.

We ended up in the almost landlocked shelter of Queen Cove, where my brother's father-in-law once ran a fish-buying scow. Of that there was no sign. Except for a bit of concrete foundation, the cove was empty of all evidence of human occupation. I began to realize that the search for my brother's memory was a little late in coming.

When we set off next morning we decided to explore Port Eliza, a long passageway that opened up on our right-hand side. Inside the entryway, in a nook to the left, was a log float and signs of a large logging camp. This sighting turned out to be fortuitous. We sailed ahead of the wind all the way to the end of the inlet, where we found what appeared to be poor holding ground for the anchor. It was now late in the day, and we decided that if we motored out into the dying wind we could make it to shelter for the night. But the motor refused to start.

There was nothing for it but to raise the sails. Using all the light-air tactics that we had learned together in racing, we worked our way out of the narrow inlet. With the last puff of the failing breeze we nosed near enough to the log float for Diane to leap off the bow with a mooring line.

The early arrival of the logging crew next morning had us out of our bunks by daylight. One of the helpful loggers removed the sparkplugs and squirted raw gas into the cylinders so that our reluctant engine would start. We thanked them and they roared off to their day's work while we grabbed a bite of breakfast. The engine promptly died. Now what?

We reluctantly decided to wait out the day, as the mechanic from the logging crew had said he'd help us if we were still in trouble after he finished his shift. After a round of boat scrubbing we were surprised to see an efficient-looking cruiser nose into the dock. It was *Port Eliza*, out of Tahsis, which belonged to Frank Collins, who owned the boat maintenance outport of Ceepeecee. On board were Frank and his wife and the clergyman and his wife from Esperanza Mission. Within minutes another boat arrived bearing Tony and Desmond Robinson, a retired Boeing mechanic. It seemed our prayers were answered. In a matter of minutes the mechanics had our engine off the boat and were taking it apart. Frank, the boat mechanic, said, "We're going to take your carburetor apart and clean it. Even if it is not the carburetor that is at fault, I guarantee you that your engine will start." And it did.

The unit was full of water and rust, picked up in that ill-fated filling at Winter Harbour. Gas is little used by the fishermen at that

Pilchard fishing off the west coast of Vancouver Island. This huge fishery lasted only a handful of years. The net is so heavily loaded that the floats are being pulled under the water.

outport because most of their engines run on diesel. For reasons of economy, the storage tanks for gasoline are often left empty during the winter, so they are almost bound to contain some condensation at the beginning of the summer. Frank added a filter to our line and that was the last we heard from the engine on that topic.

As it happened, the boaters who rescued us were friends of long standing and had planned a picnic outing. We felt like heels for using up their time, but when we apologized they waved away our concern and promptly invited us to lunch. One of the women stated that nothing made the fellows happier than solving a boat problem.

We spent the better part of two weeks around Esperanza and Tahsis Inlets. At the invitation of Frank and his wife, Linda, we visited the old Ceepeecee cannery that they had bought. This port with the odd sounding name was originally a pilchard reduction plant built by the California Packing Corporation (CPC, hence the name). The sardine fishery at Monterey had been making good money for investors, but by the 1920s things were beginning to slow down. The industry that had built the specialized oil-extraction equipment searched around for somewhere else to make a profit. In 1925, when they heard that pilchards, which are basically an oily, outsized sardine, had appeared in great quantity off the B.C. coast, there was no stopping them.

The site chosen for Ceepeecee, as the factory in Esperanza Inlet was known, met all the requirements. It was near the junction of two major waterways leading to the ocean. A large stream fed by a lake provided ample water, and there was good shelter at the dock. In short order the factory was producing fish meal to feed livestock, and oil for numerous uses—from paints to cosmetics—with no inconvenient government restrictions that required some of the fish be canned for human consumption. By 1927 there were 26 pilchard reduction plants along the central Vancouver Island shore, with shipyards, construction crews, fishermen, and shoreworkers enjoying the bonanza. Like the gold strikes, however, it was all soon over. Within fifteen years the pilchards were no more. Although small schools appear from time to time, they no longer froth the surface of the ocean in schools that once were measured by the mile.

The nearby salmon cannery was built by the Canadian Packing Corporation, a subsidiary of the California company. A large gillnet fleet intercepted fish heading up the rivers to spawn. The cannery remained in production long after the abandoned reduction plant burned to the ground. When diminishing runs of salmon meant that the cannery could no longer turn a profit, it was put on the market. Frank saw its possibilities as a service depot for the remaining trollers that still fished at the mouths of Esperanza Inlet and Nootka Sound.

Frank and Linda cleaned up the site, retaining only the dock, the slipways, the boat repair facility, and a bunkhouse that served as their residence. Frank said that when they first owned it, the fishermen had come in for repairs whenever they were needed. Now, with the shortened season imposed on them by the fisheries department in hopes of conserving salmon, these same fellows were fishing frantically, holding their boats together with bits of wire and duct tape in an effort to meet their debts before the next closure called them in.

One good thing about the demise of the cannery was that the nearby beaches were again producing clams. In the early days, gillnets were not made of nylon and had to be soaked in great tubs of bluestone (copper sulphate) to protect them from rotting after exposure to fish slime. Spills of this toxic material had effectively killed off all local sea life. But time and nature healed the wound. When we went clamming with the usual shovel, Linda laughed and handed us a rake. All we had to do was pull away the seaweed and there lay the clams. The presence of the Collinses' two large Dobermans had effectively discouraged the hordes of aggressive and sometimes violent Vietnamese clam diggers that descended on our coast courtesy of the federal government trying to find useful occupations for refugees from the Vietnam War.

The negative side of the loss of the cannery was that it signalled the end of a resource as my brother had known it in his years of fishing on the coast. The site we were visiting had employed upwards of 70 workers during each season, not including the fishermen who supplied the catch. But the salmon runs that had filled this coast with their bounty no longer existed in enough quantity to make a place such as Ceepeecee viable. Frank figured it was only a matter of time before the whole fishery closed down completely.

My brother used to say that when he began fishing commercially out of Ucluelet in 1946, all he needed was a lead line and a compass along with his fishing gear. By 1974, when he died of heart failure, his boat boasted two radios, Loran to tell him his position, and an echo sounder that printed out the pattern of the ocean floor and the shape of schools of fish. By the time Diane and I reached the area in 1987, electronic gear left the fish no place to hide but kept the fishermen deeply in debt.

We motored on to visit the mission at Esperanza. Since Diane's father had put in some years as a minister, Diane felt at home at this outpost. A religious group called the Shantyman's Christian Association had established the place, and when this group built a hospital on the site in 1937, the tiny "doll's house" first-aid station at Ceepeecee was no longer needed. The first-aid station had been run entirely on donations and was staffed by a former member of the Royal Army Medical Corps, Mr. P.B. Ashbridge, and his wife. Together they patched many a wound, extracted aching teeth, and delivered countless babies at a time when the local population numbered nearly 1,500 people. When we arrived, Esperanza appeared to be more of a summer camp for Christians who came with the intention of offering religious counsel to the Native population. By that time the

Diane with a ling cod she landed on the west coast trip.

Natives were busy rediscovering their heritage, and I am not sure how enthusiastic they were about being saved.

It appeared that the mission kitchen was running short of meat, so I rashly offered to go and catch them some fish. Diane and I set out early the next morning. I commented on the fact that we seemed to be the only ones dragging a line in the water. We did catch some fair-sized cod, one coho, and one poor undersized salmon that drowned on my line because I hadn't realized he was there. I knew I should throw him back in, but decided he'd do better feeding us than the few enterprising seagulls who had their eye on our activity.

When the fish seemed to have stopped biting, I turned back toward the mission. Diane asked if she could please clean the fish, and who was I to turn down an offer like that? M.D. that she was, she cleaned painstakingly slowly. We meandered along. As she finished I noticed a fair-sized businesslike-looking cruiser coming up behind us. It stopped a little way off and someone trained binoculars on us.

I had a hunch that it was a fisheries patrol officer, although I'd never encountered one in all my years of trolling. I told Diane to put the undersized fish in the garbage container under a paper towel in case we were boarded, and I turned to face the music.

A megaphone bellowed at us, "Don't you know this area is closed to sport fishing?"

"I've just arrived from upcoast so how would I know that?" I said. I confessed that we had indeed been trolling and I had wondered why we were the only ones.

The officer wanted to know if we had caught any spring salmon (known as silvers in the U.S.). "Heavens no," I said. "We're not that good at fishing." I went on to tell him that we were hunting for protein for the mission at Esperanza because they were nearly out of meat.

With that he said, "Oh, get out of here," and waved us on our way. I guess two women in a sailboat didn't look like much of a threat to the dwindling salmon stocks.

From Esperanza we motored back out of the inlet to the Native village of Nuchatlitz, near the entrance to Esperanza Inlet. This area reminded me of the cove in the Penrose group at the mouth of Rivers Inlet, formed as it was by a semi-circle of islets that protected us from the Pacific swells. At high tide, just enough of these swells oozed in to remind us that we were on the rim of the continent. In the evening, backlit by the setting sun, a young Native couple strolled hand-in-hand on the sandspit that connected the islets at low tide. They could have been on a South Pacific atoll, so romantic was the setting.

When we visited the small village the next day, at the invitation of two youngsters in a rowboat, we found a handsome young man carving a fine totem that he had up on blocks at the edge of the beach. He invited us to coffee in his aunt's house. The linoleum floors were scrupulously clean, as was the whole area. She explained that they no longer lived there year-round because the water supply was a problem. They had attempted to lay an underwater plastic pipe from the far shore, but the surge of the ocean swells kept breaking the line, so the village had withdrawn to a site near Zeballos. They

*The river that cuts along the back of Zeballos's main
(and only) street and its row of pioneer buildings.*

made short holiday visits to this beautiful village, carrying water from
the main settlement.

We spent a number of days food fishing out of that harbour. If
we weren't in the inflatable dinghy chasing abalone, we were out by
Catala Island looking for salmon. The whole area was a gustatory
delight. Much to our disgust, we met an American couple in a
houseboat-style cruiser who were boasting about how full their two
freezers were with crab, abalone, salmon, and cod. For us, it was a
case of filling the tummies and eking out our canned supplies.

One day we anchored by Catala Island in the bight away from
the swells. We crept in as close as possible in order to avoid a long
row to the beach. After walking the shores, we returned to find our
sailboat slowly drifting away. A hasty row in the dinghy and a scramble
to the bow and we were soon hauling up our Danforth anchor. This
proved to be an extremely heavy task. Imagine our surprise to find a
huge ball of seaweed surrounding the flukes that were supposed to
have been dug into the sandy ocean bottom. I hadn't intended a long
stay, so had been careless on that windless day.

After cleaning up the mess and moving farther offshore, we re-set the anchor, then rowed over to visit a lone salmon troller that was anchored nearby. It was the *Shaula*, which was later mentioned in Edith Iglauer's book *Fishing with John*. As we pulled alongside, I tapped on the hull and called out, "Hello, the *Shaula*."

A smiling face appeared in the doorway. "Hello yourself." It was Cliff Gissing, who told us he had fished alone for years and liked it that way because he could set his own pace. One got the impression he fished more for pleasure than for profit. It also became apparent from our discussion that he knew these waters intimately. I asked him if he had known my brother, George.

"He was a good fisherman. A hard worker and a hard drinker. I was sorry to hear that he died."

After talking about the steady decline of the salmon fishery, I asked him if he ever saved the salmon roe.

"Why would I want to do that?" he asked.

"You wouldn't need to ask if you ever tried it," I said. "Just poach it briefly in lemon juice and water to degrease it, cut it into bite-sized pieces, and dip it in soya sauce." Of course, this set me to drooling. We agreed that it had been a part of the fish that was ignored, but it didn't really matter anyway, as the fishery was dying.

As we put the oars in the water, ready to leave, he said that he had seen us having to re-anchor and advised us never to set the hook in less than four fathoms of water or it would become weed bound. He said that if we had no choice, we should search around for a spot that was clear of weeds. We thanked him, wished him luck in his fishing, pulled up the hook, and set out for Zeballos.

This town with the Spanish-sounding moniker was named for Lt. Ciriaco de Cevallos, who came to these shores 200 years before us in search of more of the gold that his compatriots had found in Central and South America. According to T.W. Paterson in his excellent book *Ghost Town Trails of Vancouver Island*, there is a report in the Spanish archives of one shipment from a source on Vancouver Island that was valued at the time at three-quarters of a million dollars.

Unfortunately the location of the find was not indicated, and prospectors still roam the hills of Vancouver Island hoping to find the Big One. Gold was discovered at Zeballos, which was thought to be the site of Cevallos's mine, and from 1938 to 1945 the area produced upwards of $13 million worth of the precious metal.

We arrived in 1987 to find this small port packed with fishing boats. In the village the false fronts on the buildings appeared to be right out of a Hollywood movie set. One almost expected to see a grizzled old miner driving his twenty-mule team down the single main street. When we entered the pub looking for a bite of lunch, we found it filled nearly to capacity. Diners found room for us at an already crowded table, and we were entertained by storytellers, each one trying to top the other.

The story that stuck in my mind took place during the Second World War, after the Japanese had all been evacuated from the coast in response to the bombing of Pearl Harbour. One night, at this very pub, revellers were delighted and surprised when one of their Japanese fishing buddies showed up with a group of his pals. The leader of the group of visitors had last been seen before the outbreak of hostilities when he left for Japan to attend his grandmother's funeral. They welcomed him with shouts and laughter and soon the table was littered with glasses, both empty and full. In the early hours of the morning the group of visitors staggered out of the bar, lugging cases of beer and saying that they had to get back to their boat. The next day, shells had been lobbed, apparently from a Japanese submarine, at nearby Estevan Point lighthouse. None of them hit their mark, making it look like more of a lark than deliberate savagery.

With this bit of speculative history to digest, Diane and I returned to our sailboat, cast off, and headed for Ceepeecee to say good-bye to Frank and Linda before continuing our trip. Frank suggested that we stop in to visit an active logging camp near Bodega Island. He had worked for this outfit and thought we'd enjoy seeing how the camp operated. On our way there I suggested that Diane edit her supply of Japanese fishing floats because our lazarette was beginning to overflow.

As we moved down that pretty, narrow waterway, a ribbon of bobbing "corks" marked our trail as she tossed duplicates into our wake.

We tied up at the float, and the camp foreman made us welcome. He told us that they had downsized recently by sending the families back to live at places like Campbell River. It had become too expensive to maintain a full-scale residential camp, so they closed the school and the loggers worked ten days on and four off so that they could go home for a visit between sessions.

That evening he took us in the camp "crummy," a fast aluminum boat, to see an ancient burial site just down the inlet. I had never travelled in one of these hot rods, and it was almost frightening. The foreman kept his eyes glued on our route and said that he could not afford to strike anything at that speed, and I believed him. Swerving around a chunk of driftwood was like leaning into the curve on a huge motorcycle.

We soon arrived at the correct indentation and he nosed the boat in to a flat rock. Hopping ashore with the line, he pointed to a cave through the trees. The single bentwood box under the overhang had long since deteriorated and broken open, the stitched-together join leaving only the row of holes. The few remaining bones showed that a youngster had been buried here amid the lonely splendour. As this site was not too far up-channel from Friendly Cove, it set me to wondering if it had been a special child to receive burial in this sheltered cove.

The foreman took us back to *Juno* and invited us to breakfast at the cookhouse next morning, promising to take us to the head of the trail that leads to the outer beaches of Nootka Island.

When we got ashore at about 7:30, only the cook and a mechanic were left in the dining hall. A table along one side held all the fixings for making lunches. The cook explained that she had the men make up their own because everybody wanted something different, but there was always a big demand for hard-boiled eggs. I asked the foreman about this when he came in for a cup of coffee. He said that the truck drivers took them to feed to the ravens. Apparently when a trucker

Child's bentwood box coffin in a cave in Tahsis Inlet.
The top right-hand corner was laced together.

stopped to eat his lunch in the cab, a raven would alight on the rearview mirror and the driver would hand it an egg. With great skill, these raucous birds carefully shucked the eggs before eating them.

We enjoyed a logger's breakfast and visited with the cook while the foreman went off to speak to the welder. The cook said that her salary topped that of her husband, who was the camp electrician. She baked all the pies, cookies, and cakes, but the bread was brought in from Campbell River. Union regulations demanded that she have three choices of entree for every meal, and she jealously guarded her system for determining what supplies she needed to order, because there were many candidates for her job, including her flunkey. The cook's hours were awesome, since the early crew in the summer had to be on the job by 4:30 a.m. and the men required a cooked breakfast. She usually took a midafternoon nap before starting to prepare dinner.

When we heard the foreman's truck return, we hurried out and scrambled up into the cab. He said he'd take us to the head of the trail and return for us around three o'clock. As we climbed to the top of Nootka Island, a call came on the radiophone about a breakdown at one of the active sites, so he dumped us off at the side of the road with instructions to keep walking until we hit the airstrip. There, at the far end of the runway, we'd see the beginning of the trail. Eventually we found the field, but we also found it to be littered with wolf scat, some of it fresh. Deer hair seemed to make up the bulk of the droppings. Hoping that the wolves were sufficiently well fed, we dropped down over the end of the rough gravel airfield and began our hike to the ocean.

One of the older loggers, a naturalist (Yes, Virginia, such a being exists!), had built and maintained the trail, complete with notched-log stairways for tough descents and handles for scrambling up bluffs. It lead out to the beach, then on down to Friendly Cove. These beach trails are all very well at low tide, when a beach exists, but at high tide the way is blocked by outcroppings of rock, and you need log steps, pull-ropes, and hand-holds to haul yourself up and over. The logger's work forms the core of the much-acclaimed Nootka Trail.

We put in a good two hours working our way to the shore, only to hear the *woomph, woomph* of helicopter blades as a party of beachcombers set off to scour yet another beach. All we found were footprints and a neat blister on my heel. Our search for Japanese glass fishing-net balls was foiled again. We sighed, sat against a log, ate our lunch, and rested. At least the view was superb—all the way to the horizon. The hike back never seems as long as the way out, and shortly after we reached the airstrip, the truck rumbled up the hill and we were on our way to the boat.

The next day, at Friendly Cove, we discovered a Native carver hard at work satisfying the tourist trade. Among the treasures offered in his shop were the elusive fishing balls, covered in beadwork and on sale for a mere $400. No wonder we hadn't found any. Native people have been experts at beachcombing for eons. In times past, the remains of Chinese junks rewarded them with metal and also fat tubes of bamboo, out of which they made lidded containers. (This information was revealed when the ancient Makah village near Cape Flattery was excavated from under a mudslide.)

We prepared to round Estevan Point with some trepidation, as John Newton's *Pachena* had been wrecked there two years previously and the father-son transport team returning the boat to Vancouver had drowned. We carefully entered a number of points in the Loran that would keep us clear of the many rocks that litter this featureless coastline. Because it is made up of low hills, it leaves you with only a vague sense of how far you are from the beach. Early morning found us on our way. Diane was monitoring the Loran and she began to notice a strange phenomenon; we were being steadily and inexorably swept onshore. The Pacific swells were just forward of abeam, and there was a huge tide running into Tahsis Inlet. It swept around the point at Friendly Cove and pushed us steadily to port.

This made us think about *Pachena*, which had been travelling the coastline at night. There had been some sort of horrendous collision, during which the father's head had received a dreadful injury and which had probably knocked him over the side. His body was found entangled in the kelp with his son clinging to him. Given the sideways drift we were experiencing, it was easy to imagine them striking a rock, with the impact tossing the father into some metal projection, then over the side. In an effort to save him, his son must have jumped into the water. The boat, made of moulded wood covered in a glass finish, was all in pieces when the search party reached the area. This had been an especially poignant loss to me as the father, Dennis Wardell, had been active in the Royal Navy Sailing Association and had been kind and helpful to me when I was a novice sailor.

That evening we were at Hot Springs Cove, soaking away the cares of the trip in the rock pools fed by the trickling spring. Since this was 1987, before there was much in the way of regulation, we found that bathing suits were nowhere to be seen. At that time there was no overnight accommodation except for those of us hardy enough to have come by boat, so in the early mornings and late evenings the stairway of pools was nearly empty. Float planes arrived from nearby Tofino by 10 a.m., so we were careful to be early or late birds.

During the day, Diane baked bread in our pressure cooker-cum-oven. (*Juno* had only two kerosene-fired elements). We simply removed the rubber sealing ring and turned the heavy pot into a Dutch oven. We found that a round, deep pan balanced inside on three metal jar rings did the job. To get the "oven" up to temperature, we first baked cookie dough in a shallow cake pan; then we knew that our pot was hot enough for the bread. We shared our goodies with a pair of fishermen who were in port, and one of them presented us with a humungous glass fishing-net ball. He said that when they were coming out of Juan de Fuca Strait that spring they had come upon a flock of these balls and had scooped them up with their nets.

As a special treat for her parents, Diane had arranged to fly them from Tofino to the cove. They enjoyed the hot springs, then journeyed with us to Sydney Inlet, where we anchored overnight. Somehow we managed to tuck ourselves into the bunks without stepping on each other. They wisely had bought minimal luggage. Next day, with Mr. Fast ably handling the helm, we tacked back out to Hot Springs Cove for another bask in the mineral springs, a feast on West Coast oysters, and a final night together before they flew back to their car.

As the remainder of Diane's holiday now could be counted in days, not months, we didn't have time to explore Clayoquot Sound, but we did stop at Ahousat because we had been told about one more hot spring we should see. This village is down a narrow estuary, and when we were there the dock and store were on one side of the channel with the houses across the way. At the wharf we talked to a pleasant young Native fellow whose hobby was scuba diving. I told him I needed a large seine-net ring to slide down my anchor line if I ever fouled the hook. (This is one way to rescue your anchor from entanglement. You slide the heavy brass ring down the line and engage the anchor at its throat, then exert a pull in the opposite direction to the entrapment.) He said he'd found all sorts of brass seine-net rings on the bottom below the float and gave me one of them. He would not accept money for this treasure. I felt I had a lot to learn about the Native custom of giving gifts.

The floating store at Hot Springs Cove in 1987, with the rebuilt Native village in the distance. The original village at the far end of the cove was inundated by a tsunami that followed an Alaska earthquake.

The anchorage at the end of this inlet looked welcoming and secure, so we dropped the hook, then rowed ashore to search out the hot springs. They consisted of a rectangular cement pool filled with tepid water that bubbled up from a spring. No one was around so we did the traditional skinny-dip and enjoyed the solitude. As the sun went down behind the trees, we walked to the sandy outer beach and found it littered with huge geoduck shells.

From Ahousat we worked our way past the zillions of crab pots, islets, and sandbars that make Clayoquot Sound a navigational challenge. Tofino was already well on its way to becoming a tourist trap, so we did the obligatory gallery crawl, spent the night tied to the dock among the fishing boats, then ran out in the early morning light through Templar Channel toward the open Pacific and made our way downcoast. We passed lively schools of herring that were being driven to the surface by hungry fish and harassed from above by equally voracious seagulls. Our choice of fishing lures attracted no attention, so we ambled on over a glassy sea with only the ubiquitous swells to keep us company on our way to Ucluelet.

Fog-shrouded fishing boats wait out a fisheries closure in Ucluelet.

My earlier summer at nearby Barkley Sound enabled me to show Diane the highlights of that islet-studded waterway. At Effingham Island we met two brothers who were completing a whirlwind circumnavigation of Vancouver Island. They had taken three weeks to do what we'd done in two months. Oh, lucky us! That evening, while sitting on their spacious aft deck, we mentioned the skeleton and the toy ball at Battle Bay. With a grin, one brother reached into the lazarette and drew out the ball, along with a glass one he'd discovered right beside it. I found myself wishing he had left the toy behind. And, of course, we envied him the glass one.

With Diane gone back to her career in Vancouver, I visited my Aunt Nora and her husband Jack, tying up at the same float by Imperial Lane that my brother George had used for all those years. I was glad of the respite from pulling the anchor every morning, and I realized I was tired from the trip. It also seemed that I had finally accepted the fact that I was retired and could now live life at my own pace.

I prowled Ucluelet roads and got to know the town where my brother had lived most of his adult life. George and Aunt Nora had both spoken fondly of George Fraser, the Scottish botanist, whose glorious plantings of rhododendrons, azaleas, heather, and exotic trees overflowed every garden. Fraser, like my grandfather twenty years later, had sought out available land and a climate conducive to specialized agriculture. Britain, where he and my grandfather were trained, and the lower B.C. coast are both warmed by tropical ocean currents that help maintain a moderate climate that is not too cold, not too dry.

Fraser came in 1894 and acquired 256 acres of land smack dab in the centre of what is now the townsite of Ucluelet. He cleared 14 acres by hand and set to work growing and breeding many different shrubs, specializing in the aforementioned species. One plant that he bred, a cross between a native East Coast wild rhododendron and *R. Japonica*, was named *R. Fraseri* by both Kew Gardens and the Arnold Arboretum at Boston.

He must have kept the post office busy because he corresponded with gardeners all over the world. My brother told me that when Fraser died at the age of 90 in 1944 there were uncashed cheques from many foreign banks tucked here and there along the walls of his cabin. He never married and his wants were simple.

Mary Baird, who has lived in Ucluelet since 1912, supplied me with more information. She said that although Fraser knew plants, he was not much of a fisherman. Apparently he went out in his skiff in hopes of catching something. Of course, she says, he had no luck, so he reluctantly turned to row back to port. He noticed some Natives who seemed to be chasing him; when they got close he found they wanted to give him a fish. He was relieved and embarrassed when they tossed a salmon into his boat, grinned at him, and paddled away.

She told me that Fraser cheerfully supplied the flowers for her wedding in 1930. He shared the fruits of his labour with all comers, played a violin with verve, and enjoyed musical evenings at this remote outpost. He donated land on which the schools, a clubhouse, and the fire hall were built. Thanks to the efforts of Bill Dale, a Saanich rhododendron specialist, and of the local Lion's Club, George Fraser's fame is now commemorated in Ucluelet with a memorial garden and monument. Also, the Saturday of the Victoria Day weekend has been set aside as George Fraser Day.

Mary Baird said that her father, W. Karn, read advertising in England about land available for pre-emption on the West Coast of Canada. He arrived in 1911 and sent for his family in 1912 when he had a house ready for them. Mary said that people from all over were coming to Ucluelet to get property. A few came in search of gold following reports of gold-bearing sands at Wreck Bay. It was almost impossible to maintain placer mining equipment given the awesome waves that hurled themselves on the beach, but there are reports that about $20,000 worth of gold was recovered. According to Mary, the rush soon petered out.

As in most coastal communities, the settlers at Ucluelet came to rely on fishing and logging for an income. Fish was either canned right there or packed on ice to be freighted by sea. Logging companies eventually had roads that snaked back in the direction of Alberni, but these were closed to public use until the late 1950s. The Second World War brought boom time to the town, as an airfield was built on flat land near Tofino and a seaplane hangar in Ucluelet.

My brother said that in the early days everyone was poor, and when company arrived you put on the coffee pot. But with an improvement in the price of fish, the arrival of a road to get fish to market swiftly, and the establishment of an Army and Navy Club and, later, a liquor store, you vied to have the best-stocked booze cabinet in town. This became his downfall. Two of his friends saw the way life was going and moved their families to Victoria, went into the sport-fishing lure business, and prospered.

Today, with logging severely restricted and the fish nearly wiped out, this outpost relies on tourism. Whale watching will last until lack of feed and pollution of the seas kill off these gentle giants as well.

Commercial fishing was already collapsing in 1987 when I was there. Large draggers had begun scraping the offshore banks clean. They came in to the float now and then, their huge nets smelly with dead krill and immature fish. In early September, between rounds of fog, I accompanied the Bairds and Nora and Jack with their boats on a three-day prowl of Barkley Sound. We spotted a foreign factory ship at anchor, lights ablaze all night while its crew processed the dragger catches.

Back in port I took art and photography lessons from Jack and generally lazed around. Soon it was mid-September and all the crew members who could have come out to help me get the boat home were involved with their working lives. I would have to finish the trip alone.

With some trepidation I returned on *Juno* to the sheltered anchorage at Effingham Island near Cape Beale, at the southeastern exit to the sound, and spent the evening programming the Loran because fog is a constant threat in Juan de Fuca Strait. Aside from entering the various points of land I had to pass, I entered the co-ordinates for the buoy at the mouth of Port Renfrew and calculated the compass heading and how many minutes I would have to run at five knots before I reached the anchorage by the government dock.

As I prepared to set out, I panicked when the auto-pilot wouldn't work. I found out that if you shut it down when the boat is heading in the opposite direction to your new destination, it gets confused. After some fiddling around I got it running and heaved a large sigh of relief. Although I prefer to handle the helm myself when sailing, the auto-pilot does allow me to attend to short tasks. Still, I always find myself hurrying from the head, pulling up my trousers as I go, because I hate not being able to see what is up ahead.

The day started out gently enough, but gradually the northwester got to work and brought with it the expected fog bank that had been lurking offshore. The wind never got much above eight knots, making it a comfortable passage except that I knew that I was travelling just inside the outbound shipping lane, and without radar there was no way I could anticipate the arrival of another boat. All commercial fishing boats have navigational aids, so I kept well inshore, watched my sounder, and stayed alert. Since the wind was coming from astern, there was no way I would hear another motor in time to avoid a collision. It was not a relaxing day.

By late afternoon my Loran announced that I was near the Port Renfrew buoy, so acting on faith I doused the sails, turned onto the new heading, and set my motor speed to five knots. A sport-fishing boat passed me on its way out and slowed to check that I was all right. I nodded and motored on, keeping one eye on my watch. Suddenly the echo sounder said I was in fifteen feet of water! Just then I emerged from the fog and realized that I was nearly on the mud flats at the head of the bay. The Pacific swells that chased me into the harbour had hurried my boat along, and my elapsed time calculations were off by five minutes.

I anchored just in from the dock, the only spot I knew about, fixed a welcome evening cocktail, and relaxed. It had been a long day, but the journey to Victoria was half over. At bedtime I automatically put the mattress right down on the floor. I had learned on the earlier visit that the evening breezes come down the road to the dock and turn your hull into the trough of the ubiquitous Pacific swells. There is nothing for it but to seek the lowest point in your hull, then lie on your stomach with one leg pulled up and your elbow out to keep your body from rolling from side to side. A fisherman later told me that there is a niche on the opposite side of the bay where I could have found relief from the northwest waves.

The sunny crispness of early morning foretold a downwind sail to Victoria. Since I had already programmed the Loran, all I had to do was eat, fill my thermos with boiling water, and head out. It was a lively run, with the genoa winged out to port and the mainsail to balance it. By 4:30 I had rounded Race Rocks, pulled the genoa around to starboard, and prepared for a reach into the harbour. By now I was thoroughly tired, and much to my chagrin I found the passageway blocked by Navy vessels out on manoeuvres. I muttered that it was time for them to go in to tea when, wonder of wonders, they did just that, falling into line on their way to Esquimalt Harbour. I had the bay to myself.

It was nearing six o'clock when I doused the sails, got my outboard running, and began to look for a place to spend the night. The first dock that showed up on my right seemed a good choice so I turned in and spotted an empty berth to my left, past a homely craft that sported a rusty anchor hanging out over its bow. I figured if I cut in just right, I would fit. As I put the helm over I noticed that the protruding hook was about to wipe out my Loran aerial, which was mounted to port on my stern pulpit. I made a dive to rescue it, forgot to put the boat in neutral, and crunched into the float. How ignominious. Slamming the motor into neutral, I hopped onto the dock, secured my boat, flopped down on the cockpit seat, and burst into tears.

Just then the female wharfinger arrived and informed me that I couldn't tie up here because it was a fisherman's float. Wiping my eyes, I told her that I had made the run from Barkley Sound alone and I doubted that I had enough energy left to pour myself a drink. She reached over, patted me on the shoulder, and said, "You stay here just as long as you want." And I did.

Venturing North

The next summer found me ferrying a friend and his wolf dog north to the Goose Islands, which are off the B.C. coast about 300 miles upcoast from Vancouver. We spent three months fishing, beachcombing, and exploring the waterways I had travelled when I was there on Paul Holsinger's boat, but this time I was the maker of decisions as my companion had only fished the rivers of Oregon. I found that as chief navigator, cook, and bottle washer I had no time to do the artwork that I craved, so I spent the next two summers back in the waters of Desolation Sound, doing paintings of boats and the glorious scenery of that area. Cortes Bay became my headquarters.

The new wharfinger there began to make life miserable for me because I often took up space at the dock that he would like to have sold for quadruple the money to day customers. In retrospect, I can see his point, but at the time, to find peace, I began exploring north of the rapids again. It is strange, but often the things that make us cross at the time—like other unwelcome events such as loss of jobs or endings of marriages—turn out to be for our ultimate good. It is a pity that we cannot stand back from the immediate present and see the long-range plan. We would waste less energy agonizing and plunge more readily into life's next adventure.

When summer rolled around in 1991 I decided to head north alone. I felt no fear because I had already travelled these waters many times, not only with Paul but also with Eleanor, Diane, and my friend from Oregon. As a side benefit of these excursions I had learned that an automatic pilot is far more useful than untrained help. Also, the mechanical pilot never argues with you and you don't have to feed it.

I broke the journey into small steps because I was in no hurry. For a change, after traversing the Yuculta, Dent, and Green Point rapids, instead of going to the next logical pass, the Whirlpool Rapids, I decided I would veer out into Johnstone Strait near Helmcken Island. I had swirled through the eddies around this island a number of times on Paul's boat when we had used the Seymour Narrows route going upcoast, so felt that they were no threat. But we had taken care to go through the area at slack water in order to avoid the powerful currents.

I chuckled later when I looked up this island in my well-thumbed copy of Walbran's *British Columbia Coast Names*. He said that when Dr. John Helmcken was being taken north in 1850 on the steamship *Beaver* (likely to settle yet another dispute between the Hudson's Bay Company and its miners at Fort Rupert), the doctor asked the skipper the name of the island they were struggling to pass. The skipper replied that it was unlabelled but he would call it Helmcken because it, too, was always in opposition.

By going out into the strait I hoped to find a way of avoiding the inevitable northwesterly that always seemed to lurk in wait for me as I emerged from the Whirlpool Rapids on the other route. After spending the night at Shorter Bay to the east, I motored out into the passage and headed west. But that day the afternoon northwesterly got an early start. As I worked my way up the northeastern side of Helmcken Island and approached the turbulence caused by the reef that juts in from the shore of the nearby coastline, I really began to feel the effects of the wind.

Over to my left I could see several fishing boats also going upcoast, but they were hugging the Vancouver Island shore as they made their way up from Seymour Narrows. I began to wish fervently I was there with them instead of out in the rapidly increasing slop at the end of Helmcken Island. What I didn't know was that most of the commercial fishermen choose to ignore the indicated traffic separation plan marked on the chart, which instructs boat traffic to keep to the right whether coming or going. The fishermen knew where to find the sheltered water.

Things deteriorated steadily. I finally decided to reef in my roller-furling headsail, as I was badly overpowered. When I am alone on the boat in heavy weather I find that I have to use the winch for this job as the line is small and hard to grip. With a stiff wind it takes a lot of strength to haul it in. Since the day had started out gently enough, I had not put on sailing gloves, and in the furor of the reefing I managed to bite a chunk right out of the side of my thumb. There was blood everywhere, but I had to secure the sail and clap on the automatic pilot before I could attempt to staunch the flow. I rinsed my hand in the swirling waters that surged past the hull, did a blotting job with a paper towel, and clapped on a bandage.

It was a nasty sail from there to shelter at Port Neville. Since it was all upwind, I had to put in a number of tacks to get there. Were I to be caught in this situation again I'd seek shelter in one of the bays on the mainland shore down the coast from Port Neville, but at that time I didn't know they existed, and studying charts with a magnifying glass is not something that comes easily when your boat is plunging along like a demented horse.

I rested at Port Neville for a day before moving on, but neglected to soak and clean my hand. Instead I slapped on some antibiotic ointment and a new bandage. Leaving it wrapped up provided the bacteria with a fine nursery. By the time I reached the dock at Sointula, 40 miles farther upcoast, I was well into a round of blood poisoning. The co-op store had hydrogen peroxide, so I alternated between hot soaks in well-salted water and dabs of that pioneer form of antiseptic. Also, I left the cut exposed to the air. My outdoor life must have kept me in reasonable shape because the infection cleared up.

Boat houses at Sointula. Fishing boats were drawn up on rails and often put into shelters for winter maintenance.

I set out to explore and photograph the remaining examples of Finnish architecture that set this port apart from others. Sointula had been one of the early attempts at pure co-operative living, but a raging fire in the main residence in midwinter killed a number of people. There was talk that the blaze had been deliberately set to destroy evidence of tampering with the account books. All this, added to the lack of reliable income, helped to undermine the enterprise.

I left Sointula one bright morning after a series of storms had eased. Near Pulteney Point I came upon a large, translucent, lime-green ball that was rolling gently in a tangle of loose kelp. It was one of a new issue of rubber boat fenders modelled on fishing floats used off the coast of Scotland. Logically enough, it was called a Scotchman. I was delighted with this find, but I suppose the poor deck hand who neglected to secure it firmly to the deck cleat had to deal with the wrath of the skipper. Since there was no name on it I laid claim and still use it to fend my boat off the dock.

I headed for Port Hardy, the last jumping-off port on the inner coast of Vancouver Island, to replenish my supplies. I had already decided to return to Bull Harbour on Hope Island and check out the Nahwitti Bar route, as I felt that the information was important enough to catch the eye of the editor of my favourite boating magazine, *Pacific Yachting*. I had already submitted one article and had it returned, so I knew that the next one had to be irresistible.

I was in no hurry. Beaver Harbour, just downcoast from Port Hardy, has always mesmerized me, filled as it is with delightful islands to explore. I return there

Juno anchored in Beaver Harbour. White clamshell beaches reflect the morning sunlight.

frequently. The Hudson's Bay Company (HBC) had located Fort Rupert here in 1846, partly because of a nearby seam of coal. Not only did the HBC need the fuel for the boilers in its own boat, the *Beaver*, but the company had also landed the contract to supply coal to Her Majesty's Navy. The many islands in the bay offered good shelter for boats, but I wondered how the company ever hoped to build a useful dock, given the sloping beach and shallow water in front of the site.

HBC employees built a sturdy fort with palisades eighteen feet high to protect themselves from the nearby Nahwitti people. The disruption of Native culture by alcohol and disease, coupled with mistreatment by unscrupulous traders and problems with communication, had bolstered the Nahwittis' reputation for vengefulness. Tales of cannibalism and riotous behaviour spice up accounts by white visitors to the area, so one can understand the desire for a safe fort.

In no time, the fort attracted more than 600 Natives, who constructed a town nearby. The population within the walls also increased when the HBC sent a group of Scottish miners to begin getting out the coal. The foreman of these workers was 26-year-old Robert Dunsmuir, who brought along his wife and three young children. In time, Dunsmuir's name became synonymous with coal production on this coast; it also labels one of Vancouver's downtown streets.

Things did not go well in this outpost. The fort was supervised by a most autocratic factor, Captain W.H. McNeill, who drove the men mercilessly. It became an unhappy place, plagued by insurrections and desertions. To top it all off, the coal was low-grade and burned more like green cottonwood than well-aged maple. When exploration at Nanaimo produced a higher grade of coal, this northern mine was abandoned.

By 1873 the company sold out to its manager, Robert Hunt, who had married a Native princess and raised a large family. Although the fort was destroyed by fire in 1889, the store was still in operation in the 1920s when the cruising Pinkertons arrived there one summer to visit Mr. Hunt's descendants. What Kathrene Pinkerton learned from George Hunt's wife helps to explain why the shore was paved with a two-mile-long band of clamshells, which was reported to be 50 feet deep. Mrs. Hunt was braiding cooked butter clams onto sticks so that she could smoke them over beachwood fires. These intricate plaits of dried shellfish served well in the winter when low tides are always at night and clam digging in the inevitable rain is a miserable task.

Deer Island, which is opposite the site of the old fort, is carpeted in daisies and foxgloves with grassy patches and trails throughout. The remnants of wartime gun emplacements remind you that the nearby airfield was part of the coastal defence system in the Second World War. There is little undergrowth on these pretty islets, as salal, which usually chokes the spaces between second-growth trees, does not seem to thrive here.

Granddaughter Casey amid the wild flowers on Cattle Island.
She and her mother visited every summer wherever I wandered.

On a blazing hot summer day I anchored *Juno* in the bay and rowed to the glare of Shell Island, which is so white with discarded shells that it looks like one itself. There I found wild black "currants" begging to be picked. I had no pail, so made do with various plastic containers that I found along the shore, all the while surrounded by the ghosts of Native women and children who had harvested these richly flavoured berries before local stores offered commercially prepared jams. In no time I had picked enough to fill an ice-cream pail. Because the berries were almost sun-dried, there was no rush to process them. I did not have a suitable cooking pot anyway, so I waited until I got back to Port Hardy, where I could borrow a large stainless steel one from the crab lady at the float. Soon there were jars of currant jam to share with her.

There was a wealth of boats to sketch or paint at Port Hardy, so I bought a month's moorage and was able to tie among the many fishing boats that waited there for an "opening," at which time they were

My painting of fishing boats "quadruple-parked" at Port Hardy.

allowed a 48-hour orgy of setting their nets. My coming and going in the 25-foot C&C had attracted a bit of attention, unbeknownst to me. With the deep sailboat keel, a transom-mounted rudder, and outboard I was able to dock with panache. I always found that in backing up I could face aft and picture my rudder leading me, so I looked like a pro as I tucked myself into seemingly impossible spots.

When quiet weather arrived I left for Bull Harbour, stopping along the way near the downcoast end of Hope Island to enjoy the anchorage at the deserted Native village by Kalect Islet. This had once been a large settlement. My chart, first issued in 1948, indicated at least eleven structures. All but ten of the inhabitants died in the flu epidemic of 1919. When I first went there in 1980 nothing remained except the odd trade bead in the pea gravel of the sloping beach. By the time I returned in 1991, a scuba-diving charter boat had used this feature to attract customers, so the beach was stripped. Because the weather was quiet, I anchored right out in front of the grassy

Roller Bay at Bull Harbour on a rare calm day.

village site, which had a breathtaking view across Queen Charlotte Sound in one direction and toward Vancouver Island in the other. At times I have seen fishing boats tuck into the narrow pass that leads to the inner lagoon. No doubt they had ridden out southeast storms with their stabilizer poles stretched out on each side like the legs of a water beetle.

When I motored on to Bull Harbour next day, I found a greatly reduced coast guard staff on site. On my first visit there had been families present, and the intrepid fellows were wrestling with dreadfully outdated radiophone equipment (shades of the early days of lighthouse keeping, when the isolated government employees nearly starved on poor pay and lack of support services). Now the few workers that remained came in on a rotating schedule. Those I spoke to were helpful when I asked them about the Nahwitti Bar. They said they never had to try my bypass route because their vessel was geared to handle bar crossings, so they couldn't comment on it one way or the other. But they did recommend that a skipper planning to cross the bar should go out of Bull Harbour into the channel and have a look. If you could see the horizon you knew that the breakers were manageable; if not, you should return to port.

I paused to enjoy the harbour before doing my research. There is a huge eagle nest on Norman Islet at the mouth of the bay, and the current fledglings were still hanging around it. As I went ashore to explore the midden site, I pulled my rubber dinghy up over what appeared to be plain bladderwrack. Much to my distress I found the big barnacles that lurked beneath did a great job of scoring the hull. In time these deep scratches peeled back, and the ultraviolet rays were able to destroy the cloth backing. I didn't get around to making a dinghy cover until much of the sun damage had been done. I also found that some of the barnacles on the midcoast can be as large as teacups and are razor sharp. They formed the bulk of the diet for Natives in such places as Fury Cove, at the mouth of Rivers Inlet, where the beaches are stark white and prickly from discarded shells. The meat, which was poked out of the shell after it was steamed in a firepit, looks for all the world like scrambled eggs, but likely tastes better. (I gathered my test sample off a creosote piling, so was reluctant to eat it.)

Loitering around Bull Harbour, I had time to do a painting of the tiki-like rock formation that marks the fairway past Norman Islet. I thought it would serve as an illustration for my upcoming article. (In September 1992, when *Pacific Yachting* did print my article, it reproduced the painting in black-and-white, which left me feeling that I might as well have painted in sepia. It was years before I discovered that the publisher had great difficulty reproducing the colour of artwork. In time I learned to do my own negatives by photographing my paintings outdoors, out of direct sunlight. The lack of blue light indoors distorts all the greens and blues.)

When I had done all I could around the harbour, I set out to verify what I had learned the year Diane and I circumnavigated the Island. After checking compass headings for the crossing to Vancouver Island's shore, I followed the route Diane and I had taken inside the line of kelp that marks the edge of the Tatnall Reef as we hugged the coast and made our way to Sutil Point. Once again I noticed that the current was negligible, and even the Pacific swells were diminished. This was definitely an improvement over crossing the bar in rough conditions. I interviewed fishermen who told horror stories of actually hitting bottom during a particularly big swell and of having their heavy batteries break loose with the jar of the impact. Satisfied that I had enough material for my article, I retraced my path and went back to the anchorage in Bull Harbour.

There was a sockeye fishery due in two days, so all the net-fishing boats would be coming north to crowd the anchorage, leaving lots of room at the dock back in Port Hardy. I decided to make the 23-mile run south in order to do the laundry. Next morning I heard on the radiophone that a gale warning had been issued. Strong north-westerlies were expected. The air was still and it was sunny—no sign of a northwesterly—so I opted to loiter on the way instead of huddling in a sheltered cove. I stopped to check out the usefulness of Shushartie Bay as a possible anchorage. Except for a few rotting pilings along the right-hand shore, there was no sign of the dock or the old cannery that my cousin Rod Griffin had told me about.

I had hoped to find something here because I had read Gloria Morrisette's manuscript of her early teen years spent at this bay. Gloria's father, Norman Godkin, had brought his wife, three daughters, and young son here at the close of the First World War in hopes of finding a place to settle and prosper. Gloria says that they arrived on the Union Steamship in the middle of the night and were dumped off on the wharf with all their belongings. Her father had been told there was a hotel nearby, but when they enquired of the postmaster, who was waiting on the dock to receive the mail, he told them that he had a sort of rooming house at his store and that was the only shelter available. They had no choice but to climb into his boat and go across the bay in the dark. I am sure that Godkin was crestfallen, and I can only speculate on his wife's comments.

At that time, the Goletas Cannery was still active and operated for a few more years, so there was seasonal work available. The Godkins struggled along in a rented house, trying to establish themselves in this out-of-the-way place. They made a bit of money catching fish, but finally gave up and moved on, as had previous settlers.

During the 1940s a shipwright by the name of Scholberg settled here. My cousin Rod Griffin said that Scholberg had worked in the Victoria Shipyard, helping to build the five-masted, bald-headed schooner *Malahat*. This handsome craft, with its powerful auxiliary engines, freighted lumber overseas before joining the large fleet of rumrunners during the American prohibition years. It ended its life as a log barge carrying Sitka spruce from the Queen Charlotte Islands to Teakerne Arm in Desolation Sound.

Scholberg took his earnings and struck out on his own, locating his business amid the timber and the fisherfolk at the far end of Vancouver Island. During the 1930s he built boats at nearby Cascade Harbour, where Brown's Sawmill cut all his lumber. But when the postmaster's job at Shushartie came up for grabs, he moved his household and works yard over there. This cut out the often perilous trip to the Union Steamship dock to receive his shipments of engines, shafts, kegs of nails, and other bulky equipment needed for boatbuilding. He lived with his family in a two-storey house and established a new yard where he produced some of the finest fishing boats on this coast, among them the *Skeeter II* and the *BC Troller*, which are both still in use.

The boats he designed and built were stunning, with a graceful flare and sheerline and a deep hull, a fisherman's dream. As a youngster, Rod visited one owner of a Scholberg boat while in Bull Harbour. The old fellow said, "My boat has been around a long time and it may be 'nail-sick,' but all the fittings for the bow roller, mast-step, and metal bracing show not a sign of pits or rust. When Scholberg finished these he heated them red hot, then plunged them into dogfish oil, which annealed them, keeping them young forever."

Rod said that he went back to Shushartie Bay when he finally got his own troller and found the house, the boat yard, and a shed stacked with well-aged edge grain lumber. The place had obviously been deserted recently because nothing seemed to have been disturbed. He never did find out what had happened to this skilled artisan. Certainly the demise of the Union Steamship Company in the early 1950s would have helped empty remote settlements such as this. The trail to Port Hardy was a poor substitute.

I motored around for a while, inspecting the shoreline for signs of habitation, but found none visible from the water. It appeared that anchorage would be possible at the head of the bay if you really needed it. Shushartie was named by local Natives and means "place where the cockles are." No doubt the beach was littered with these tasty morsels. And according to my friend Joe Christensen, the mud also contains two bronze cannon. I didn't feel I could use those, so, turning the boat, I meandered out into the fairway, only to be greeted by the first puffs of the approaching gale.

Some winds arrive politely and some hit you full in the face, as did this one. Sorry, weatherman, I should have believed you. I turned to run before it with just the genoa out. Adding the mainsail would have provided more power than I wanted to handle. Because the tide was running out in the opposite direction to the wind, it wasn't long before the seas built up into steep waves. The first fishing boats began approaching me, heaving brilliant spray from their bows on their way upcoast. I headed over toward the left side of the passage, ready to duck into shelter among the many islands that I would have to bypass on my way back to port.

All of a sudden the lower end of my genoa began peeling away from the track. I dove for my safety harness, put the auto-pilot to work, clipped myself onto the safety line that ran along the deck inside the shrouds, and worked my way forward. The shackle that held the bottom corner of the genoa had lost its pin. I had to go below, search out a spare, remember the wrench, and go forward again. Speed was essential because if the sail pulled out any farther I would have a hard time getting it back in the track, yet if I hurried I could fall over the side. The steepness of the waves didn't make the job any easier.

I glanced to the right and saw a whole flock of boats passing me, bashing spray but doggedly heading upcoast. I couldn't help thinking that the new government policy of telling the men when they could fish put many of them at risk. I was out in this by choice (or foolishness), while they were there trying to earn a living.

What I didn't know until much later was that they were all worrying about me and discussing my strange activity on their radiophones. I have no doubt that had I gone over the side I would have been rescued. This is one of the distinct advantages of the buddy system. People like the Pinkertons and Muriel Wylie Blanchet travelled this coast when it was alive with people. Every nook and cranny had handloggers or settlers trying to wrest a living from a hostile environment. Except for the occasions when there was a net fishery going on, I sometimes went hours without seeing another boat. My only hope, if I went over the side, was that I would remain conscious, be able to work my way aft, and reach the string that I had tied at deck level in a large bow so that I could drop the boarding ladder and climb aboard. Or, should I drown but remain tied to the boat, the coast guard would not have to hunt for my body.

I enjoyed a real sleigh ride on my way back to port, but I had to duck in close under the lee of the shore at Duval Point, where I paused to reef in the headsail before sailing broadside to the wind into Port Hardy's harbour. Fortunately docking was a cinch with the area empty of boats.

After a harbour day I returned to Port McNeill on the inside coast of Vancouver Island. My friend from Cortes Island, Nellie Jeffery, then in her 70s, came up by bus and joined me so we could explore various deserted Native village sites. Nellie has a keen interest in Native culture, so it was a treat for her to visit the many sites chosen by the midcoast people for their homesites.

I had shopped for groceries before she arrived. The first night out I was too tired to mess around cooking the frozen chicken pieces that I had in the icebox, so we had steak. Next day we poked around into various bays and inlets off Blackfish Sound. That evening I found

The cliff at Echo Bay with a floating community along its base.

to my dismay that the chicken was beyond recall. In desperation I put it in the flying-saucer crab trap and we attracted enough crabs to more than make up for the lack of chicken. Anyway, who wants fowl when they can feast on Dungeness crab?

Nellie had heard from her son Barry about the beauty of Echo Bay, so we set out for that remote port in a vigorous northwesterly. For someone who never sailed before she met me, Nellie was a demon for speed. It was a good thing I had traversed this waterway many times before, because we roared along, giving me little time to study charts. We had to tack into Echo Bay itself so that I could furl the sails in the shelter of the point. Fortunately the dock near the school was deserted, so I tied up there. Both of us were awed by the grass-covered midden that appeared to be more than ten feet deep, evidence that the Kwakiutls had lived here for many years.

Echo Bay is truly the home of the echo. There is a handsome steep cliff opposite the low point that houses the marina. Sounds tumble back at you, drawing your eye up to the heights. Clear patches on the rock face are marked with red ochre symbols, the meanings

Looking back from the shoreline of Village Island.

long forgotten. What remains is the legend of a nearby mountain cave that is said to be the cradle of mankind.

On our return down Retreat Passage we crossed over into Knight Inlet, to Mamalilaculla on Village Island, where the Englishwoman Kathleen O'Brien had built a hospital for tubercular Native girls, as well as a school that got its supplies from the Department of Indian Affairs in Ottawa. Her work is carefully recorded in Doris Anderson's fine book about the Anglican Coast Mission, *The Columbia is Coming!*

The float home belonging to Kathleen O'Brien and Eleanor Nixon. It was towed to the Village Island beach by the Columbia *in 1926.*

*Kathleen O'Brien's sanatorium that she had built
at Mamalilaculla to care for tubercular Native children.*

A more recent delightful publication, *Totem Poles and Tea*, tells the
story of a young teacher/nurse, Hughina Harold, who worked there
in the early 1930s with Miss O'Brien and her helper, Kate Dibben.
John Antle of the Anglican Coast Mission firmly believed these small
schools that allowed children to stay with their families were much
better than the huge residential schools that did so much to destroy
the culture, and time has proven him right.

We explored the decrepit sanatorium, enjoyed the ample crop
of raspberries, photographed the totem that remained standing,
admired the huge house posts, and walked the beach. As usual, the
site faced the sun, with an ample clam bed on the beach in front.
What struck us was the proliferation of bits of broken china. Scraps
of porcelain from many dinner sets littered the shore. Nellie observed
that the Indian agent must have had his hands full supplying the reserve
with new sets of dishes.

I told her there was no point in looking for artifacts as I had
walked this area many times and never found a thing. That said, I
looked down by my foot and there beside my toe lay an adze made
from sleek, greenish-black stone. At some point its edge had been

partially shattered, but it remained a work of function and beauty.

Before moving on, I rowed Nellie to Grave Island. I had been there years earlier with Paul. At that time grave robbers had raided all the mausoleums and ghoulishly arranged the skulls in rows along the remaining sills. At a later date, young Native people built cinderblock containers above the shoreline and placed in them all the ancestral bones that they could find. I wanted to show my friend the intricacy of the grave houses, ranging from ones built of wide, straight-grained virgin cedar fastened with square handmade nails to later humble log cabins or even split-log structures.

These mausoleums were the result of European restrictions that discouraged tree burials, where the dead were placed in their personal bentwood box and tied high above the shore in the arms

The "White man's pole" got its name from the hatted figure carved at the summit. It was one of the numerous totems that gave Village Island an aura of mystique.

Native skulls (one appears to have been bound in infancy) amid the berry bushes on Grave Island at Mamalilaculla. Handmade square nails held the planks that formed the walls to this particular mausoleum.

A cast-iron cooking pot rests beside a shed at the deserted village site of New Vancouver in Knight Inlet.

of trees, which, in turn, were remarkably healthy due to the nourishment that came from above. There had been insufficient soil in the area to allow standard European burial techniques, so the dead were put in coffins that were placed in small communal structures. Someone had retrieved a few missed skulls and again arranged them in full view. One old skull sloped back above the eyes and had obviously been bound into the desired shape in infancy.

After our visit to the island we motored over to New Vancouver, which had been a dying settlement when Hughina Harold visited it years earlier. When we anchored in front we saw a large black bear amble out onto the beach and begin turning over beach stones. He was searching for small crabs to supplement his diet of grubs and berries. We didn't think he'd appreciate competition from us, so we decided an early lunch onboard was the smartest thing to do. We ate and watched him through the binoculars.

When he finally strolled away we clambered into the dinghy. There was no sign of totems as there had been at Mamalilaculla, but among the ruins we did find a large, cracked, cast-iron cooking pot. These had served the early logging camps, where dogfish livers were rendered in twenty-gallon pots heated over an open fire to extract the oil that was needed for greasing the peeled logs on the skid roads. They had also been much treasured by Native chefs because they eliminated the need to lift rocks from the firepit into carved wooden bowls in order to boil water that waited therein. There was no thought of taking the pot with us, partly for a practical reason: where would you store a 24-inch container on a small sailboat? Also, it seemed only right to leave things for future explorers to enjoy. Unlike Mamalilaculla, this village site was a sad, dreary sort of a place.

We returned to Port McNeill and I put Nellie on the bus and then was joined by Margery Walker. I had first met Margery in Cortes Bay. She was another single-handed sailing woman, except Margery was one up on me; she truly was single-handed. She told me that her husband had died when she was in her 60s and she'd had to search around for some outdoor activity that she could manage on her own. Together they had canoed and tented over much of the province, but she could not see any way to handle these activities alone.

At the age of 65 she learned to sail a Sabot dinghy in a class held at Comox. When she felt sufficiently knowledgeable, and with the help of a mentor, she bought a 23-foot Ranger sailboat with a simple mainsheet arrangement, which she kept at Schooner Cove on Vancouver Island. The outboard engine did not have to be hauled up out of the water, merely tilted on its arm, and the jib was small so tacking was easier. She found anchoring worrisome, as do most newcomers to coastal boating, so she went from dock to dock. Ultimately her hours spent on the water daysailing out of Schooner Cove probably far outstripped those of any other boat at her marina. She also caught her share of salmon.

Her sailing nephew from Ontario sometimes joined her, but those were the only times she got to explore beyond the area of Desolation Sound. I offered to include her in my upcoast explorations and she courageously leapt at the chance. I felt honoured that she would want to join me. Together we planned to explore Seymour Inlet, which had finally been properly charted. For years the shape of most of this area had been indicated by vague dotted lines. Tugboat men knew it well, and a few intrepid skippers ventured in, but the rest of us stayed away.

She arrived by bus and next day we set out across Queen Charlotte Strait on the 35-nautical-mile journey to the Southgate Group, which is a cluster of islands along the mainland shore upcoast in the direction of Cape Caution. We spent the night in nearby Allison Harbour. My old map indicated docks and extensive facilities at this sheltered inlet, but nothing remained except ghosts, one of whom was a local woman who had been so generous with her favours that the loggers in Seymour Inlet re-named her the A-frame.

During those days, alcohol was banned in the camps so stills were hidden here and there in the bush. Bootleggers probably made better money than did the loggers. Also, the ever-helpful storeowner in Allison Harbour sold quantities of lemon extract and Aqua Velva shaving lotion to meet the cravings of a steady stream of customers. As I heard it, to get the alcohol-rich lotion you had to buy the whole shaving kit. The bobbing trail of discarded shaving brushes on the route back to camp must have puzzled the local seagull population.

My cousin Rod came to this area in the early 1940s as a whistlepunk, the lowest of the low in a logging camp. It was his job to pull a jerk wire on a steam donkey engine in order to produce a whistle that sent a signal to let the loggers know the next move. As a youngster, he was sent to bunk with the fallers, a group of Swedes and Finns, who were the elite of the camp, next to the high-riggers. When Rod stripped down to his brand-new set of Stanfield's woollen underwear, one of the old-timers said, "Son, you're gonna learn to love them itchy grey bastards. No matter how vet or cold it is, you'll always be varm and dry."

I'm sure Rod was a welcome addition to any camp. Even as a youngster he was a natural-born storyteller with a tremendous sense of humour. He also played the accordion with skill and could sing all the popular ballads of the day plus the many songs he had learned as a youngster while he attended the dances on Cortes Island.

In Seymour Inlet he worked at the Kerr and Dumaresque camp. He said that watching the loggers waterproof an expensive new pair of leather caulk boots was an education in itself. They cut off the end of a 45-gallon drum and filled it with oil rendered from seal and bear fat. Then they suspended their precious boots in the oil to soak, but were careful that it didn't run over the top and get inside. Even so, their socks and feet were guaranteed to be greasy for days afterwards. But the boots never leaked a drop.

During the original timber harvest in Seymour Inlet (where the total shoreline is said to measure more than 500 miles) there were about a dozen logging camps. These were housed on floats, with each outfit employing upwards of 60 men. There would also have been a regular flow of tugs with flat booms of massive logs navigating the hazardous Nakwakto Rapids on their way to the mills downcoast.

Slipping through the gap by the Southgate
Group of islands, bound for Allison Harbour.

My first visit to Allison Harbour was in the early 1980s with
Paul Holsinger on his small wooden sailboat. After we set the
anchor, a pair of motor-driven inflated rubber rafts zoomed
toward us. The occupants asked where to find the dock so they
could set up their tent. We told them the dock was long gone,
and I suggested that they could camp on the beach, as the tide
would not be very high that night. They responded that they didn't
trust tides. When I asked to see their chart so I could show them
a good place to go, they handed me a B.C. road map! They were
visitors from Germany, had rented the rafts in Port Hardy, and
were determined to go fishing at Rivers Inlet. How they would
tell when they reached that magical spot I had no idea. Maybe
they expected to find a road sign.

Paul and I moved closer to the rapids the next day, anchoring in
the tiny bight below Cougar Inlet so we could observe the turbulence,
but we did not venture into the inlet itself, which was largely
uncharted. Margery and I did have charts, and because slack water in

the narrows was early the next morning, I decided to go to the same small anchorage beforehand.

Once again, my only reference was *Cruising Beyond Desolation Sound* by John Chappell. The chart shows two possible approaches, the main one being Slingsby Channel. Schooner Channel is an insignificant-looking passage that starts right by the entrance to Allison Harbour and joins up with the larger passageway just below the rapids. Chappell implied that the current in Schooner Channel was negligible, so I blithely set out, only to find that we were being sucked rapidly forward toward the narrows. We passed a large cruiser coming toward us, and its passengers looked at us in shocked surprise. I watched for the turn into our planned anchorage and heaved the tiller over much in advance, put the engine at full throttle, cut through the ridge of water, and sliced into the shelter with much pounding of heart. I had maintained a casual visage because I did not want to panic Margery, but I'm sure she saw through my bluff. When we were settled I looked up the current reference in the book of tide tables and found that both channels were clearly rated, giving the maximum amount of flow plus the time of change when the water was briefly still. The route I chose showed an approximate speed of four knots when I so foolishly plunged into it. I saw the error of my ways. Oh dear! In the long run, one's fate is one's own responsibility.

Next morning we went out into the remains of an opposing current, lingering around the mouth of Cougar Inlet while we waited for the flow to abate. There seemed to be little slack time, because we found that when we did venture in we were already being swept forward by the water that had decided to hurry along in the opposite direction. We turned left and soon passed a floating logging camp where children ran out onto the logs as we cruised by. Among the buildings was a greenhouse, which struck me as a most intelligent innovation. Not half a mile past the camp a small bird lit upon our rigging. I wondered if the children had tamed it.

On the far side of the dogleg bend in the channel where Seymour Inlet becomes Belize we could see across to Lasseter Bay, which looked

Juno *tethered below a cliff in Alison Sound, where a huge bear crashed through the bushes in the evening.*

like it must have a huge sandy beach because it gleamed so brightly in the morning sun. The binoculars revealed heaps of bleached logs and snags tumbled together. It left me thinking that southeast winds must howl down this long straight waterway in the winter and that many a boom of logs had gone astray. Cape Caution is just over a low point of land, so we found ourselves beating into a stiff northwest summer breeze as we worked our way toward the bend into Belize Inlet. We were glad when we could make the turn and run down this handsome passageway. Our trip became a treat with the genoa winged out on one side and the main balancing it.

We furled the sails for the turn at the spectacular entrance to Alison Sound. Sheer cliffs, glacier scraped and water stained, rose first on one side, then the other. The narrows, marked at three knots, looked lively, but we swept right through and on toward the Indian reserve on our right. I motored close by to read the depths, as it looked attractive with its sunny exposure. We were fairly close to shore before I got a reading of 40 feet, so we decided to move on. Past a narrow, sharp point we came upon a beautiful spot. A tall cliff towered to our right with huge rocks broken from its face littering the shore. The chart showed an underwater rock to the north so I dropped the hook clear of it and backed in toward the mouth of the marked creek. To keep us from swinging into danger, I fastened the stern line to the tentacles of a gnarled uprooted stump that had come to rest on the bank of the stream.

There was no wind here and the air was warm, so we took turns having sponge baths in the water that bubbled across sun-baked stones on its way to the ocean. I felt as though I were sliding back into my childhood, when baths in summer were a rarity, living on a boat as we did; they were an occasion to be savoured.

After supper we lounged on the back deck, watching the indigo shadows creep up the rock face with the sea reflecting the magnificence as only it can. While we sat entranced, the bushes suddenly began to shake in the path of a body crashing its way up from the stream and across the bottom of the rock fall. There was no attempt at stealth so it could only have been a large bear. We were grateful that it had waited till we finished our baths and were back on board.

In the dark of night I went out to check our position and found a ribbon of stars above but total blackness down in our abyss. All was still so I returned to my warm bed. Some anchorages keep you alert, but some bring you a great sense of peace, as did this one.

Next morning found us at the beach again as we anticipated a short day's travel ahead of us. Margery volunteered to burn our paper scraps, and I wanted a picture of the boat in the early slanting light. As I came back from a search for animal tracks I was delighted to find her deep in a tai chi manoeuvre on the shore. What a mesmerizing spot to find peace!

After breakfast we set off to enjoy the beauty of Alison Sound. Since there was not a breath of wind we cruised slowly along the shore, where I found a fine rock painting in Summers Bay. The white, lichen-free rock faces chosen by early artists can usually be seen from a distance, so I make it a practice to search them with my binoculars.

This ancient Native rock painting of a three-masted square rigger (upper figure) is located on a cliff outside the entrance to Alison Sound in Seymour Inlet.

This red ochre drawing showed a large canoe with a standing figure followed by six canoes side by side. Whoever they were greeting must have been suitably impressed, as were we. There are numerous reserves noted on the chart, so these waterways must have boasted quite a Native population at one time.

Summers Bay, with its mud bottom, looked like a good anchorage but was deep until close inshore, so we went around the point to another bay, which was more sheltered from the persistent northwesterlies. The water was as warm as the air, and since *Juno*'s cooler was only insulated from above, the ice began to deteriorate rapidly.

Next day we returned down the passageway. As we turned west to re-enter Belize Inlet I spotted another Native rock painting on the shore to our right. This one showed what was undoubtedly a ship of the structure of the *Discovery*, bearing three masts with crosspieces. Near it was a pinnace with numerous oars and a figure seated at one end. Our curiosity was piqued. Had Vancouver (or Drake before him) actually negotiated the Nakwakto? We drifted nearby, took photos, and marvelled at the durability of this bit of history.

Before long a puff of the approaching daily wind urged us to be on our way, so we powered up again, retraced our original route back past the Nakwakto Rapids, and headed up Nugent Sound. At Holmes Point we spotted the Native house that Muriel Wylie Blanchet spoke of in *The Curve of Time*. It had seen better days and was choked by berry bushes. I could not resist a look so dropped the anchor and went ashore. I climbed to the top of the island and found the soil to be loaded with clamshells, the first I had seen in this waterway. There were two small beaches, one on either side of the island, a few chinaware scraps, and glass fragments but not the usual array of junk, so this had been home to a careful, tidy family.

My old early chart ceased beyond this point except for dotted lines suggesting the shape of things to come, whereas our brand-new chart was most encouraging, so off we went. Nugent Sound was disappointingly plain. Perhaps we had been spoiled by the glory of Alison.

We travelled on until we got to a narrows where the current notation left us a bit apprehensive. Did they really mean 78 1/2 knots? We decided that the depth marking was simply too close to the speed notation and that the current was really only half a knot. However, the northwesterly wind was by now in fine summer form.

We anchored for the night near the entrance to Schwartzenberg Lagoon, where I went fishing. Many huge dogfish finned their way around the lagoon outfall. One monster was nearly five feet long and looked as large as a sturgeon. Not wanting to tangle with one of these behemoths, I rowed across the bay to a rocky outcropping. There I soon caught a nice sculpin for our supper. The longer you are away from port with a rapidly warming icebox, the more time you must spend chasing protein. It's a pity we couldn't eat the large horseflies that arrived in hordes.

The next day found us approaching the rapids again as we made our way into another finger of this splayed-out waterway. We prowled up Seymour Inlet itself, which turned out to be a long fjord. As it was definitely northwesterly season, I did not relish going all the way to the end just to tack our way back, so we overnighted part of the way

Fog drifts down over the slopes in Seymour Inlet.

along in Warner Bay, which is fed by two lakes and a lagoon. The water was deliciously warm and I went for a swim before heading out on another fishing expedition.

We got up early the next morning in an attempt to outsmart the wind. No such luck. We tried to find shelter in a large bay opposite Harriet Point, but the land was low and the wind howled right through. I moved back up the channel behind a finger of land and found sanctuary behind a small islet. As we were turning into the bay a kingfisher startled us when it hit the water nearby with the force of a thrown rock and bounced right back up with its beak full of dinner.

After settling the boat, I went for a dinghy prowl and was able to haul a good supply of water back from a rocky stream bed where there were neat little pools, just right for bathing. I find these pockets now and then and wonder about the people who built them.

Next day we moved slightly back toward the rapids and anchored in Charlotte Bay in good mud. It looked like clam country so I took Margery ashore with me, but we found that large bears had been harvesting cockles by picking them up from

A derelict net boat in the fog on the Southgate Group
is a reminder of a fishing trip gone wrong.

beneath the beach grass and bashing them open on exposed rocks.
Broken shells and huge footprints surrounded each outcropping.
A hasty return to the dinghy seemed in order. Leaving the rest of
the clams for the bears, I got out my fishing net and we scooped
up rock crab instead. These tough-shelled creatures are so scrappy
that you can even antagonize them with a stick and they'll hang
on long enough for you to heave them into your boat, but you
better be wearing shoes instead of bare feet when you dump them
on the floor of your dinghy.

Having had our fill of Seymour Inlet we went back out through
the narrows to Allison Harbour. Here we woke to find the life lines
decorated with ghostly spider webs bejewelled by droplets of water.
Fog had arrived during the night. It lifted enough by midmorning
that I felt reasonably sure we could work our way downcoast to
Blunden Harbour. I had now traversed this waterway a number of
times and the shorelines had become as familiar as my backyard.

We wormed our way through the narrow gap into the Southgate
Group, but I lost my nerve to go any farther. We anchored near the

shore in five fathoms, well down behind the cluster of islands that gave us some protection from the swells. Margery found scrambling over rocky shores difficult, so I went ashore alone to look around and came upon a streamlet that formed pools as it tumbled down to the sea. Robert Frost's poem about cleaning the pasture spring always comes to mind when I find a water-gathering pocket along this coast, and like Robert, I stopped to clean it out. I rowed farther along and came to another, only this one was different. The rocks here were smooth, with two shallow natural basins that filled before overflowing and running down into the sea. On a clear summer day the water would likely be warm.

Just above them and overhung by delicate branches was a larger pool that enchanted me. Water spread in a veil over a rounded wall that glowed with the iridescent green of wet moss. It dribbled into an oval basin that appeared large enough to seat about five bodies around the edge with their heads above the surface. No doubt it would be cold through most of the year, but in the summer and fall on a hot day it would be tepid, as the flow of water was not all that fast. Was this a work of nature, a ceremonial bathing place used for Native ritual cleansing, or did a frustrated tugboatman prepare it as a diversion while waiting for calm seas? It seemed too breathtaking to be the latter.

I returned to the boat for water-gathering supplies. The two collapsible plastic containers usually live up to their name as I try to fill them, but I did get some water back onboard, and the kerosene heater kept out the damp while we reclined on the bunks to drink tea and read the day away.

We woke to more fog, but it was definitely thinner so I elected to move down to Blunden using the shore-hugging route. I still had no radar, but the echo sounder coupled with careful chart reading usually got me where I wanted to go. Now and then I doubted my homemade deviation table and worried that I had shifted some metal object nearer to the compass since the calculations had been done, but usually I found that faith in my own abilities was reasonably well founded.

Most of the trip found us skirting the edge of the shallows. Now and then we had to set our course across an open patch that led to a narrows where we inevitably met other boats. This route was one of the major shipping lanes for upcoast traffic, but the day was windless and we were not sailing, just plugging along with the outboard running, so I was able to stay on a set course. All we had to deal with was the occasional boat wake and the heart-stopping sight of a huge tug and barge emerging from the shadows and quickly disappearing.

I had trolled for salmon so many times around the entrance to Blunden Harbour that the return had a definite homecoming feeling. Nevertheless it was a relief when we finally were able to drop the hook and call it a day.

Fog plagued us off and on during the 25-mile trip across Queen Charlotte Strait to Port McNeill, where Margery caught the bus home, and it didn't give up even when my friend Anne Reilly arrived to join me for the trip home.

Anne wanted the experience of coastal travel. I had met her in Vancouver the winter before when she asked if I could teach her how to sail. When I asked her why she wanted to learn she said that when she knew how she'd buy a boat. I replied, "No, no! You've got it all wrong. First we pick out the right boat and then you can learn to handle that particular vessel. There are lots of knowledgeable, boatless people who will go out with you for a day's sail."

I knew that the older model of C&C 25 was a solid, easy-to-manage boat for a beginner. We set out to find one. As luck would have it, *Appleseeds* was on the market. The owner had used it in Lake Ontario for a number of years. Now a job transfer to Vancouver and the arrival of a second child made a larger boat imperative. So there we were: a freshwater boat with non-corroded through-hull fittings and well-maintained in the bargain. Anne took the plunge and never looked back. She told me that when she joined a class of younger students in a local sailing school she, the 58-year-old woman, had been shuffled out of the way and the youngsters got to do most of the things that mattered. On her own boat she learned with alacrity.

*A cruise ship greets us as we emerge from the fog
at Blackney Passage just above Robson Bight.*

Anne was an intelligent, courageous woman who already knew
how to fly a plane, but the job of head night nurse at Richmond
General Hospital had taken its toll on her health and she needed
fresh-air experiences to undo the effects of stress. She knew nothing
about the water or sailing but had the spirit to take on this new
adventure. Our trip downcoast would be her total immersion in
sailing, anchoring, and coastal navigation.

We waited around Port McNeill for several days in dense fog.
Finally a morning dawned when the fog seemed to be breaking up,
so we set out, only to find ourselves completely enshrouded within
minutes of leaving port. (Will I never learn that fog lifts and descends
at will?) I had a good echo sounder and the Loran, so felt no great
anxiety. Yes, it would have been nicer to be able to see where we were
going, but the tide was with us and there was no wind. With Anne's
excellent hearing we were safer than I would have been alone, deaf as
I am. I found that I could confirm where we were by observing the
sudden arrival of swirling currents coming at us from the port side as

The old log store and post office at Port Neville speak of busier times.

we passed the various islands between which the water funnelled as it hurried down toward Johnstone Strait. I hugged the left side of the fairway so we would clear the mud banks opposite Alert Bay.

There was a brief glimpse of the marker on the corner of Cormorant Island, and a few vessels with radar passed us on their way into the docks at Alert Bay, but we carried on. We knew we were alongside Hanson Island because the currents were behind us, although still strong. Suddenly we burst out into the sunshine, only to be greeted by the bow of a huge liner emerging from Blackney Passage on the left. No doubt he'd known all along where we were, but the arrival of his bow came as a distinct surprise to us. We were in no danger of a collision, but we courted heart failure all the same.

The currents were so favourable that we made a quick trip of the 43 miles to Port Neville, one of my favourite spots, mostly because of the warm hospitality of the Hansens. I first visited there in 1980 on *Saffron* with Eleanor Frisk as crew when Ole Hansen still sold fuel and gave you water if it wasn't too dry a season. There is a lively current past the dock that keeps you alert while docking, but other visiting boaters are always willing to lend a hand with your lines.

One fall I found myself completely locked in there by gillnetters when a fishing opening was due that evening. On one vessel two men were working hard on their supply of beer. A dark-haired boy who must have been about five years old was part of the crew. He spent the day playing on the beach and dock and generally keeping out of the way of his parent. Lorna, Ole's daughter, was most concerned for his safety because their Labrador had recently died and a cougar had taken to coming right into the front yard of her house. Together we watched over the child. I fed him and gave him a toy truck that I'd found on one of my beachcombing forays. At six o'clock all the boats had left but his. I asked him where his dad was and he replied that he was asleep, so I suggested maybe it was time to wake him up and tell him that everyone was gone.

A fierce southeast wind kept me locked in port all the next day, but the fishboats remained out there dealing with it. Some of them came in after the fishery was closed down so they could catch a few hours' sleep. They told me that most of the small boats try to cling to the Vancouver Island shore so that passing ships can go around them. This explained why we were entertained during much of the evening by enormous vessels passing close to the harbour entrance, but according to the fishermen a foreign cruise ship had cut through the fleet during the night, causing untold damage to their nets and catch. Since all such large vessels must carry licensed B.C. ship's pilots, this transgression is hard to understand. It may be that the awesome wind and frightful conditions had pushed a few boats farther out into the fairway than they realized. Whatever the reason, my sympathy was with the fishermen who were driven by debt and constrained by time. Perhaps the same could be said of the large ships.

That summer trip with Anne held no such drama. Usually drama is the last thing you want on a cruise anyway. Anne had already begun the extensive round of Power Squadron courses, which she tackled with a sense of purpose. She was taken aback by my method of determining courses. Yes, I did use the dividers and parallel rule, but no, I did not calculate true north. I used the inner circle of the compass rose, which showed the variation typical of the area we were traversing. On such short courses I could see little sense introducing room for arithmetical error when the calculations were already done for you. As a trained pilot she craved accuracy, but I wasn't searching out some distant airfield.

I also taught her my non-standard anchoring technique, learned while single-handing *Saffron*, in which I lowered the anchor over the side and waited for the boat to stop. Later, with a proper chain locker on the bow of *Juno*, I did the same thing, except in this case the boat travelled forward until the anchor snagged. Then the stern swung around so that the bow faced back in the direction I'd been travelling. Single-handing requires different techniques than when a boat is fully crewed. But since this method had never let me down, I could see little point in changing it when I had help onboard.

I think a journey like this is perhaps one of the best ways to learn boat lore in general. Not only did we face many different sailing and anchoring conditions, but we also dealt with the problems of coping with a limited supply of water (wash the dishes in salt water), keeping the interior dry (boil the pasta on an outside burner), and keeping warm on a cold day (fill a thermos with hot water in the morning so that instant soup or hot drinks are readily available).

We both enjoyed the trip, Anne because of the things she learned and I for the congenial company. It also confirmed my suspicion that women guests always do more than their share of the chores and are rarely offended at having to take direction from another female.

Pacific Yachting had accepted my article on bypassing the Nahwitti Bar, so I decided to combine explorations of newly charted waterways, which I could write about for the magazine, with trips to entertain my various women friends who otherwise would never get the chance to make these journeys. Since I was retired, time was no longer a restriction. Winters became a time for planning great adventures.

Dog Days

A newly issued chart of Smith Inlet drew my attention in the spring of 1992. I had made good use of various anchorages in Smith Sound, just past Cape Caution, but had lacked the courage to explore its deep fjord, which had been outlined only by vague dotted lines.

The chart wasn't the only new arrival that spring. A Welsh terrier puppy became part of my crew. The year I turned 63 was the first time I had lived totally alone. My musician son Ian, who had come home to help me with my aged father, finally moved into his own digs. All that remained was the big white cat I had found at the SPCA to keep my dad company.

Although a cat is a good companion, it is hardly a watchdog. I found that when I removed my hearing aids at night I was almost totally deaf. Living in a ground-floor suite left me feeling vulnerable, and getting a small dog seemed the best solution to my problem. My intention was to train Susie to become a "hearing-ear" dog, but my choice of breed left me with a self-assured, independent little lady rather than a helper. I was able to train her to respond when the phone rang, but she did it entirely at her own speed.

I was pleased to find that while we were aboard she didn't keep the whole marina awake with her barking. A quiet "woof" alerted me

Susie at two months with the white cat. Susie obviously misses her mother.

to the arrival of visitors, but a hail of barks rang out when she heard an otter under the dock while we were walking along the floats. I guess the violent splashing of an otter had frightened her when she first heard it, but her response stayed the same. Certainly her priorities bore little resemblance to mine. However, I did enjoy the companionship.

Susie's presence on board changed my boating habits. I had always enjoyed exploring new beaches, but now there was no element of choice. I thought I had her trained to use a piece of Astroturf on the side deck, but once she discovered the joy of sniffing new shores she could hold out for twenty hours until I gave in. When I finally arrived at an anchorage she would jump up and down on the soft floor of the inflatable if it was still lashed upside down on the foredeck, treating it like a trampoline until I untied it and dropped it over the side.

In fair weather she wore a body harness and I leashed her to a clip amidships in the companionway. To give me a greater feeling of ease, I laced some strong seine netting from the toe rail to the life lines. This resurrected salmon net was sturdy enough to keep me on board as well.

When the outboard was running on sunny, windless days, Susie preferred to lie along the side deck as far from the racket as the line would allow. During her first beat to weather she wanted to be in my arms because she was afraid of the noise made by the sails during a tack. As a single-hander this obviously left me helpless, so I had to send her below. After she got used to the noises she preferred to be in her crate anyhow, because there she could gnaw on her leather chewy and nap the trip away. I had never owned a dog and truly enjoyed her voyage of discovery as she learned how to become a member of the crew.

Susie is in her preferred spot for motoring over silken seas on Juno *as we approach Robson Bight from downcoast.*

Susie and I set our course for Port Hardy that year because Margery Walker was due to arrive by bus. We planned to explore Smith Inlet using the newly issued chart. The 140-mile trip went quickly, and since I arrived a few days early I hung around Beaver Harbour for a while, trying my luck at fishing. The first morning I woke to fog but figured I could still do a spot of trolling. My sounder reported plenty of activity below the hull but I had no bites.

I thought about that one for a while and decided that if the fog obscured my vision it was likely doing the same for the fish. I put a silver flasher on the line, followed by a white flashtail lure, and kept the line just below the surface. In no time a good-sized salmon took the offering. It fought for a while, thrashed right up on the surface,

*Susie trying to get her teeth into a salmon
I caught at Beaver Harbour near Port Hardy.*

then dove below and dragged its heels. When the belly finally showed alongside my hull I sunk the gaff hook in behind the head and the line parted at the lure. With a mighty heave I landed a 36-inch female spring salmon. But what a shame to have caught her and wasted all those eggs!

Susie was delighted and tried to take a bite as soon as I had the fish immobilized. She ended up washing the body with her tongue in eager anticipation.

Since I had kept Peel Island in sight it was easy to get back to my favourite anchorage. I cleaned and stored the fish and took Susie for a run on shore. By early afternoon the fog appeared to lift so I set out for Port Hardy, once again miscalculating and having to inch my way along from point to point with one eye on the sounder and one watching for kelp beds. I would never have done this had I not been confident of my knowledge of the area. Even so, stress kept me wary and my eyeballs burned from straining to see.

Port Hardy was plugged with gillnet boats getting ready to leave the next day for a fishery opening at Smith Sound. Meanwhile, the fog that began the day before became thicker. You could see it falling in drops, making dimples in the murky water of the harbour. That was not all that hit the water. Tins that had held bamboo shoots, canned milk, and beer floated around and tinked against the hull, while plastic bags and other flotsam left me shaking my head in amazement. The old-time fishermen seemed to be the worst offenders, growing up as they did before recycling became a cause. Perhaps the level of alcohol in their blood while in port also left them careless.

When they all departed for Smith I knew we'd be seeing them again. In those days it was hard to find a time in the summer when fishboats weren't hanging around the major spawning areas. Some people, like the Jordan family from Cortes Island, spent their summers anchored in places like Smith with other fishing families. The kids rowed between boats, explored together, and did their share of the chores. Boats took turns making the run to port for supplies or else waited for the fish packer to arrive with milk and groceries. In earlier days, before refrigeration, these inlets were seasonal home to many cannery workers as well. Smith itself had plants at both Margaret Bay and Hickey Cove, so the fish were processed almost immediately. In those days there was always a store at these sites where fishermen could buy groceries on credit.

Back in Port Hardy the floating electrician was up to his neck making urgently needed repairs or installing the latest in fish-finding gear, while pubs and restaurants struggled to keep up with the demand. Deck hands and cooks rolled down the aisles of stores, filling shopping carts to overflowing and dragging along a second or third cart that was equally jammed. It was easy to share a taxi as there was a steady stream of them heading for the fisherman's dock, saving me the long hike from store to wharf.

Margery arrived July 14. After one more quick run to the stores we set out at midday for Smith Sound. At five knots I had no intention

of making the 40-mile crossing in one hop; we headed for nearby
God's Pocket. The tiny bay was full so I carried on past Scarlett Point
lighthouse, intending to anchor in Clam Bay on Nigei Island, but the
weather was so quiet that we continued to the old village site at Kalect
Islet. The only drawback to this spot is the current in the nearby
channel. It can build up to five knots and has to be factored into your
travel plans.

The next day I regretted that we hadn't used the gentle weather
and gone right to Smith. It would have made a fairly long trip, but at
least we would have been there instead of getting stuck at Kalect Islet
for two days while a northwesterly gale blew itself out. "Seize the
day" should be a boater's motto.

The third day I again woke to swells rocking the boat. I wormed
my way back down into the sleeping bag until it was time for the 6
a.m. weather report. Environment Canada said that the winds were
10 knots at Scarlett Point but were expected to die down, then rise
to 30 to 35 knots later in the day. With a bit over twenty miles between
us and Egg Island, we decided to make a run for it.

We emerged from the pass into swells left over from the gale.
They were big and ugly and came from just about every direction to
boot. With no wind to fill our mainsail, which would have steadied
the hull, we pitched and tossed around miserably. Susie was locked
safely inside her crate, which, in turn, was jammed with a bundle of
life jackets in the passageway to the head. By the time we neared
Cape Caution the new wind hit. I unfurled the genoa and the boat
settled down. We were glad to be sailing, as there is no joy to be had
while slogging along under power in turbulent seas. All this time
Susie had been quiet but utterly miserable. When I finally rescued
her from the crate she had thrown up and wet her bed and could
hardly wait to get off the boat.

We ducked into tiny Jones Cove, just past the Cape. For years
this slit of a harbour had been home to a Millerd Brothers floating
fish camp, which serviced a large Japanese fleet of gillnetters that
worked the area near Egg Island. All that is left of this enterprise is a

*Packers tied to the lone piling at the mouth of
Jones Cove, just in from Cape Caution.*

lone piling by the entrance. We arrived in the bay to find that we
were not alone. Although the fishery was in full swing, boats came
and went for quick repairs, a short rest, or a visit to the packer
anchored at the entryway. There are times during a lull in the fishing
you can literally walk from shore to shore on the decks of waiting
boats. They tie four to an anchor when the wind is down, and now
and then at night you wake to a quiet thud and have to go on deck to
fend off a hull as the tide turns all the boats around.

I was glad that I had a small rubber dinghy that would fit on the
bow of my boat and was light enough to heave over the side when I
needed to take the dog ashore. There was no seat in this tiny boat so I
had taken to kneeling astraddle a boat fender while facing forward to
row. This position had two advantages: I didn't get a kink in my neck
from twisting round to see where I was going, and the bow rode up
farther onshore so Susie and I could jump out right onto the beach.
While Susie sniffed around I often watched the family of eagles that
made this their home. They had become unafraid of humans. The
fishermen would sometimes toss them bits of fish and offal, and the
birds would swoop down and grab the food before it sank out of sight.

On one trip back to the boat a large eagle glided toward the bow,
intent on relieving me of my puppy. I struggled to unlatch one of the

I row ashore, straddling a boat fender and facing forward. Susie is ready for a beach adventure.

Eagle bait.

The fish packer Lumeral *waits to buy fish while at anchor in McBride Bay, Smith Inlet.*

oars so I could take a swing at him, but at the last moment he veered away and grabbed a seagull that was bobbing nearby. The other eagles joined in the raucous game, all trying to snatch the squawking gull from the talons of the predator. During one particularly lively scrum the gull fell into the woods in a tangle of feathers, and the eagles soared off over the trees. I knelt in my dinghy, clutched my dog, and shuddered.

We woke to fog, a usual summer hazard around the mouth of Smith Sound. While waiting for it to lift we had a leisurely breakfast, then motored on to look at Margaret Bay, near the junction of Smith and Boswell inlets. There was no longer any cannery in sight and there appeared to be minimal shelter from the northwest wind that was pushing the fog away, so we turned to the right and powered through the mist to anchor in McBride Bay.

The head of this bay is closed off by a handbuilt rock wall that forms a fish trap, ready to snare the salmon aiming for the moderate-sized stream that murmurs into the ocean from under the trees. The water within the pool was quite warm and would make a dandy place for kids to play. The farther north you go, the more often you find these Native fish traps, perhaps because logging has disturbed those to the south where the soil seems richer and the trees larger.

Although the water looked inviting, I felt no urge to swim on a foggy day, when the damp creeps through your clothes and drips from the rigging. We were joined that evening by a small fish packer, *Lumeral*, which dropped its hook near the point. I made a sketch of her the next morning as the new day swept the fog up the inlet, then I rowed over to have a chat and to accept their ready offer of chipped ice for my cooler.

After breakfast Margery, Susie, and I set off to explore nearby Ahclakerho Channel, which leads back toward Smith Sound. Fishermen told us that they sometimes pushed their way through the narrow channel right on into Smith Sound, but often as not they clipped their propellers en route. I took this whole story with a grain of salt as it looked impossible, but I guess with enough booze and high spirits the young ones would try anything.

We ventured carefully into Ahclakerho and I soon found that the boat was being swept forward at a good clip. With all the obstacles in the way this seemed like a poor idea. I turned around and beat a slow retreat. Back at the mouth of the channel we dropped the hook in Anchor Cove. Later in the day we rowed over to interview a fisheries officer who had anchored his comfortable craft nearby. He towed a large inflatable with a huge outboard engine, so his big boat was obviously his home during the season.

A knock on the hull brought him on deck and he filled us in on various local attractions. He said the Ahclakerho runs up to six knots during big tide changes and that I had been wise to give up. The newly issued chart made no mention of current. I included a note about this for the article I was preparing for *Pacific Yachting*. The fisheries officer also told us what would greet us should we go to the head of Smith: horseflies by the millions. I had long since lost my enthusiasm for runs up long fjords in the summer, when I would invariably be faced with a return beat into the ubiquitous afternoon inflow winds, so I quizzed him carefully on what to expect and left it at that.

The fisheries officer also told us where to locate water in the area. He said that the fishermen had rigged up hoses at two locations. We went to check them out. *Juno*'s tank only held five gallons, leaving water high on our want list. One source was in a narrow gorge at the entrance to Waysash Inlet. There is a log tied across the bay with a green garden hose draped over it and an empty plastic bottle tied near the end of the hose to keep it afloat. A mooring line is fastened to the log and you can secure your boat to it while filling your tank. The water was brownish, as is much of the water in that area. We quickly did a small laundry in the cockpit, rinsed things thoroughly, and left with clean clothes and a cleaner boat.

The other water source was just up the inlet from McBride Bay, where Gordon Lake empties into the saltchuck. I fear with the fishery drastically curtailed that these simple facilities will fall into disrepair. I'm sure that people like the Jordans worked on the water systems when they first arrived in the spring. With a family of six on the boat they'd have gone through a generous supply each season.

We holed up in front of the old cannery site at Hickey Cove while a powerful northwester shredded the outer channel. Onshore the mud was lumpy with bricks, each named for one of the many coastal factories that flourished in the early days all the way down past Seattle. I even found some from Clayburn, where I had raised my family. While hopping from grass clump to brick, Margery found an old ceramic Chinese wine jug. (There was always a China House located at these canneries. These labourers were not allowed to bring their wives or families into the country, so they lived in barracks with their own cook.) With the variety of boats and workers that congregated at these places during the season, there were bound to be many treasures lurking on the bottom.

On the opposite side of the bay there was a net-mending float like the one in Margaret Bay, but since I am not a diver and cannot

Juno *coming into Boswell anchorage.*

check the condition of underwater linkages, I always feel better swinging on my own hook.

We awoke to calm seas and powered to Boswell Inlet, where the wind finally built up enough to give us a neat run to the narrows. This dogleg is an artist's delight, with attractive rock formations and delicate trees screening the turn. Although the breeze was still with us, there were no whitecaps up the length of the channel. We turned to the left after the narrows and tucked into a small, unnamed bay where my anchor set right away. It was as well I hadn't dragged it around at all because it became apparent that this had been a logging site. Underwater debris is always a hazard at these places.

When I took Susie for a run I found to my dismay that loggers had left the entire shore a tangle of rejected scrap. Trees in this part of the coast tend to grow raggedy crowns called cathedral tops, so there is a lot of waste left behind when the straight parts are removed.

Since the beach was a mess, Susie had to make do with a patch of mud, but the view up the inlet with the receding march of ever bluer peaks kept my camera happy.

We wound our way back to Jones Cove through the usual maze of bobbing white float corks as the gillnetters laced the inlet in a final attempt to snare the salmon on their way up the many streams that drew them onwards to the spawning grounds. The fishery ended that evening, and I counted 117 boats that came within my line of sight. I'm sure most of them joined us in our haven. When the usual gentle thud wakened me at tide change, I lashed the rubber dinghy across the stern to protect both my outboard engine and the Loran aerial and returned to my warm sleeping bag. I'm sure the exhausted fisherman hadn't heard a thing.

When we left Jones Cove we found a ten-knot headwind lurking outside the bay, so we made a long tack past Egg Island, turned, and ran downcoast, ducking into skinny Miles Inlet, which nestles between the two possible entrances to Seymour Inlet. Although this was a short run from Jones Cove, we welcomed the shelter as the wind began to pick up in the afternoon. Being retired has its perks; I no longer had to battle heavy weather unless I felt up to the challenge.

Otters have made the point of land at the T in Miles Inlet their home. Their leavings have built up the soil in amongst the jagged rocks, and the grass forms a thick mattress filled with intriguing smells to entertain Susie. During the blustery afternoon we were joined by another boat with children on board who soon went off to explore the lagoon that feeds into the passageway from the west. Both crews were glad of the respite offered by this little arm of the sea.

Next day found us back in Port Hardy with Margery off home on the bus. The port was filled to the brim with both seine and net boats that had returned from the grounds while we hung out in Miles Inlet, so I reluctantly paid the extra bucks to tie at the shaky docks offered by the local private marina.

This marina, like many on our coast, was chock-a-block with sport-fishing boats, all intent on catching as many salmon as possible.

These people came in their mobile homes, complete with what amounted to a mini commercial fish cannery. The wives worked the pressure cookers while the fellows went out to harvest the fish. Visitors went back home with cases of canned salmon and full freezers. I heard one woman boast that she paid for her entire holiday with what she processed under the awning of her camper.

With our fisheries department struggling to keep the streams stocked with fingerlings, and our fishermen cut back to a few days of work a year because of stock depletion, I felt anger whenever I beheld these so-called recreational fisherfolk putting such a dint in the supply. They reasoned that they had paid a hundred dollars for their sport-fishing licence so they had a right to be there, but the working fishers depended on the business to feed their families, and their expenses far outstripped those of the sport folk. I am aware that statistics show a greater financial return to the province from sport fishing, but this wholesale canning goes far beyond the realm of sport. Since my time upcoast, regulations were put in place that forbade the recreational canning of salmon. Now these marinas have begun to feel the same pinch as the fishermen.

Meanwhile, down at the wharf among the sport boats I swallowed my anger and set to work on engine maintenance. Although the Honda outboard was supposed to recharge the battery as it ran, no recharging seemed to be happening. I found the batteries to be low in water. As well, the hook-up to the motor was exposed to splash from the ocean, and the terminals were corroded. I find that most electrical problems on my boat are related to dirty connections due to the constant exposure to salty moisture. Even the masthead light suffered this fate. The problem was never the bulb but always the dirty contact points.

An oil change came next on the agenda, so I set to work on that chore. In the late afternoon, when I was cleaning the grease from my hands, I heard a call from a nearby boat. My neighbours suggested that it was time I settled down with them for a late-day cocktail. As they had a jolly Scottie dog on board, Susie thought this was a good idea, too. During the introductions it turned out that one of the men, Fraser Gavin, had spent part of his life at Cortes Bay, the Blind Creek of my childhood. I was introduced to Georgina, his wife, and to the Keans, who were their cruising buddies from Powell River where they all had their homes. They travelled together in their two boats for many a summer's adventure, but were stalled at Port Hardy waiting for parts as one of the boats had suffered a breakdown.

Fraser was particularly impressed with my apparent skills of boat maintenance, but I told him I had learned from the many people like him who had helped me solve problems over the years. I wouldn't have ventured so far north if I hadn't had a fair amount of knowledge.

The weather was lovely the next morning, and since it was just mid-August I decided to revisit the many beautiful waterways that thread the coastline off Queen Charlotte Sound on the mainland shore. On a bright windless morning Susie and I departed Beaver Harbour below Port Hardy and motored past Numas Island on our way to Wells Passage, which is the first fjord that cuts into the mainland below Seymour Inlet. Off Numas I spotted what appeared to be two large logs bobbing upright in the water. These navigational hazards are called deadheads and oftentimes lurk just below the water's surface, but I was puzzled to see two so close together. I cruised nearby and woke a pair of disgruntled sea elephants, who snorted and dove out of sight. Some logs they turned out to be! I wish I had put the binoculars on them ahead of time. Then I could have caught the huge pendulous snout of the largest one on camera. He was truly a nautical version of Jimmy Durante.

As we swished into Wells Passage on an incoming current, we passed numerous sport-fishing boats working along the northern shore. I assumed that they were headquartered up-inlet at Sullivan Bay, but soon learned that quite a few of them were from boats holed up behind Dickson Island at the entrance to the passage. I had visited this spot years before on Paul's wooden boat when we were the only craft around, so was taken aback to find a number of others there. Times do change. Someone had even put lines at intervals along the shore to provide tie-ups for stern lines. This is commonly done on the lower coast in a well-used small bay when there is not enough room for the normal rotation of numerous boats swinging at anchor.

We found an unoccupied spot and settled in. Before taking Susie for a walk, I rowed over to a boat anchored nearby. The vessel looked comfortable, solid, and well-used and was registered in Campbell River. Canadian boats are rare in this waterway so I wanted to say hello. I introduced myself to Henry and Grace Peterson and asked them about the anchorage. (Chappell had listed it as suitable in settled weather only.) Henry said the tie-ups made all the difference and that he had sat out a 40-knot southeaster here with no trouble.

After talking fishing for a while, I left and went across the passageway, looking for an interesting spot to walk Susie. We landed on a patch of beach by the mouth of a stream and found a small midden site. The shallow streamlet was about the right size to attract dog salmon in the spawning season, so families before me had enjoyed this bit of shoreline, too. One of the unexpected joys of taking a dog on a boat was finding the many bits of history that I would likely never have discovered before she joined the crew.

Up until now, any trips I had taken alone were strictly for the purpose of getting the boat from here to there. Now I was beginning to enjoy exploring with the dog. I decided to venture into nearby Drury Inlet because I'd never seen it and the chart looked intriguing. I noted in the log book that the rock at the entrance was flat and wide. There was also a big tide running in and it was *fast*.

We anchored in Richmond Bay, where I found a mixed collection of rocks all tumbled together on the beach. Probably they were the melt debris from a long-ago glacier. I lugged a particularly heavy one back to the boat because it looked distinctly like a chunk of petrified wood, something I had always wanted. A geologist from Simon Fraser University later identified it as a sample of riverbed that had been pressed well down into the planet, become cooked and bent, then been returned to the surface in some prehistoric upheaval. He was glad to get it as a specimen, and if it wasn't petrified wood I didn't want it. My lazarette was pleased to be unloaded of its weight and bulk.

Susie and I explored farther into Drury Inlet, stopping for lunch at the Muirhead Islands. The one marked 195 on the chart had a small bay with a pebbled, clamshell beach and a three-foot midden on a well-sheltered bench facing south. Loggers had cut a tree using notches for springboards so they could get above the tough butt wood, leaving a stump that measured seven feet in diameter. We rambled around under the cover of the second growth and found many more stumps. The island had obviously been well forested at one time, and no doubt it had water, too. I also noticed when I returned to the beach that the predicted northwest wind was a gentle southwest here. Maybe the Farmer Hills protect these islands.

With four feet of keel hanging down below my hull, I decided not to try traversing the narrows that led farther inland. I lacked an extra pair of eyes to look out over the bow and warn of shallows. (Dogs are handy but not *that* useful.) We anchored for the night in a bay in front of a logging camp and left the inlet next morning. I went on to explore many of the anchorages that I had visited years before when cruising in Paul's wooden sailboat. Certainly there were many more boats. Bays where we had been alone now held four or five boats, all much larger and grander than my 25-foot sailboat. At Sullivan Bay we were positively dwarfed. Tenders were larger than my humble craft, and the women on board had not a hair out of place or a broken fingernail.

I found out why when I decided to treat myself to dinner at the Greenway Sound Resort. Amenities offered to visitors included a beauty salon and a reminder to the "girls" to bring their colours. I must admit that no one seemed startled by my bedraggled appearance, although my single-handed boating did attract attention.

The floating resort was not connected to the land, and the docks were handsomely carpeted, with doggy "piddle parlours" located on smaller attached floats that were so wobbly they gave my juvenile pet the willies. A man off a huge cruiser with an equally large dog asked if he could borrow my dinghy to take his dog for a walk up the trail on a nearby beach. I was in the process of launching the inflatable for

Susie but could hardly refuse him, nor did I feel capable of managing his hound. Consequently I offered him both my boat and my dog. That proved to be a bad decision for she must have eaten something revolting on her walk. About three in the morning she demanded to get off the boat and proceeded to paint the carpeted dock with quantities of runny diarrhea! I spent the pre-dawn hours with a deck bucket and broom trying to erase the evidence. Radiating guilt, we scuttled away at first light. Back to the beaches for us.

We explored all the old familiar haunts and several new ones. I couldn't resist clamshell-laden beaches because these were invariably situated at beautiful sun-warmed locations. With a northwest gale predicted, we ventured into the shallow inner bay at Joe Cove. A sturdy log float offered a picnic table marked with the Western Forest Products logo. I found out why the next morning when two logging families arrived from Port McNeill for a weekend visit. They politely let me know that their people had installed three such floats in the Blackfish Sound area, but that I was welcome to tie up as long as I left room for employee boats, which usually arrived on weekends. They helped me shift around to the other side of the dock to make room for their larger hulls, and we all enjoyed our stay, especially Susie because they had brought her a playmate in the form of a rollicking pup.

With the arrival of fall and shorter hours of daylight, I returned to stock up at Port McNeill and pointed the bow homeward. By now I was feeling confident about using the push offered by the various rapids, so surged through the Whirlpool Rapids on a gleeful run down through the Green Point Rapids to Shoal Bay. There we met the usual round of autumn fog followed by five days of violent southeast gales.

Shoal Bay made a pleasant stop, what with the grand panorama of Phillips Arm spreading out before my eyes. The old buildings that remain on shore lean tiredly together and offer but a hint of the hustle and bustle of this port in the early years of the twentieth century. With two stores, a post office, two hotels, restaurant, and ballroom

SHELTER FROM THE STORM

SHELTER FROM THE STORM

*Mining engineer Charlie Disney boarding the electric train
used to bring quartz ore to the dock at Shoal Bay, c. 1930.*

complete with ladies of the night, it would have been a magnet for
men from the many logging camps that surrounded this area.

There was also an active mine that used pack mules and, later, an
electrically powered train to carry quartz ore down to the waterfront
to be shipped out for processing. This port became the distribution
centre for mining outfits that dotted the slopes in all directions,
making lots of work for the assayer, Mr. Farquhar, in his office at
Shoal Bay. As early as 1898 there were four regular Union Steamship
visits per week, bringing in supplies and ferrying passengers to and
from both Vancouver and Comox. Unfortunately for those of us
wanting a glimpse of history, the surviving Shoal Bay Hotel burned
to the ground in the summer of 2000.

One afternoon at the dock a grey pigeon settled in under my
canvas dodger. After a meal of sunflower seeds it moved right inside
my boat. The pink and blue leg bands it sported suggested it must
have been someone's pet, but the wharfinger knew nothing about it.
I'm afraid that its uncanny ability to poop on my boat upholstery

made me unwilling to become its parent. Besides, I kept busy enough cleaning up the float after my young dog. I discussed my problem with the owners of a comfortable older vessel that arrived, and they agreed that with two dogs, a pet rabbit, and an ancient cat already on board, one more pet would hardly sink their craft. They promised that they would advertise the find when they got back home, so I gladly passed along my freeloader.

The storm that held me there abated, followed by the usual autumn fog. It lifted one morning when my patience was at a low ebb. I studied the current tables while sipping a cup of tea. If I left soon, maybe I could go through the Gillard Rapids and run the Yucultas in the last hour of the flood. It was not a huge tide, so the flow would be manageable. Should I take the risk? A check of the weather forecast made up my mind—another frontal system was rolling onto the coast.

I readied the boat, started the engine, and cast off. If I got there too soon I could always dawdle around behind Horn Point before tackling the Dents. As I motored along I thought about the forces that fuel these currents. The inrushing water struggles to get through the passes to fill the Strait of Georgia basin, all the while being pushed along from behind by the rising tide. This deep-sea tide has already begun to fall before the job of filling the strait is complete. Since the Dent Rapids are nearest to upcoast, they feel the lessening of pressure first. The water slows and begins to retreat while the Gillard and Yucultas, a couple of miles upstream, are still trying to finish their job.

I reasoned that I had to use the last of the current if I was going to make it through all the rapids in one go, so I plunged into the Dent with some determination. It wasn't too bad, mostly swirls and eddies with no whirlpools to curl my hair. As I approached the constriction of the Gillard a huge cruiser out of False Creek in Vancouver overtook me. It slowed right down and gave me a lot of sea-room, which I acknowledged with a wave. I don't know if the boaters were calling to me on the VHF because mine was off. I can only hear it when the engine is quiet and I am wearing headphones. The cruiser scraped along as close to the opposite shore as it could.

I kept well to the right and was hurtled toward the gap. Just as I cleared the light, two large cruisers roared across my bow, struggling against the awesome current. They must have come from Big Bay and been swept out of my sight when they were caught by the flow. The nose of my boat buried itself in their turbulence, then shot up like a cork. Water gushed into the cockpit through the gap in the transom, the hatch slammed back and forth, then my motor quit. I skied along, balancing on the bulge of the crest. Roaring eddies rushed back on my right toward the narrows. Oxygen filled my brain, surrounding me with Technicolor images, and I knew that if I panicked I was gone.

The road of the current opened up ahead of me. I gripped the tiller, struggling to keep the keel in line with the flow. As the force eased I glanced back at my lazy motor to see if it was still with me. It was, with the fuel line dangling uselessly over the stern. It had popped free of the engine, but the fitting was still intact so I steered with my knees, blew the water from the connection, attached the hose, squeezed the pressure bulb, and pulled the starter rope. The engine gave an apologetic cough, then roared to life. "Welcome back, little friend." I glanced down at the tiller between my thighs and chortled.

The large cruiser was almost out of sight ahead, but now I knew why it had held so far over to the left. The crew must have known of the pair of approaching boats. As for me, I had a fleeting memory of my friend Mike FitzJames, who had said of the Kitsilano trestle, "Always approach an obstruction well out into view. You have to let the other guy know you are there." Yes, Mike, you were so right. I had forgotten that rule and almost paid for it with a collision if not with my life.

I headed down into the womb of Von Donop anchorage, not to emerge until next day.

Doing the Johnstone

Back home in Vancouver I set to work writing about Smith Inlet for *Pacific Yachting*. Much to my delight, the article was edited by none other than Sven Donaldson, who had become a staff member. His style matched mine so closely that there were no bumpy passages as sometimes occur when your editor uses a different turn of phrase. I had begun to realize that each of us has a personal form of "music" in our writing and our speaking. Lucky is the author that finds an editor who writes in harmony.

To illustrate the story I did a watercolour of *Juno* coming into the snug anchorage in Boswell Inlet, using my sketch and photos as a guide. When the article came out, the picture was reproduced in black and white. The magazine limits the number of coloured pages because of the costs involved and I was one of the unlucky ones, but since all the other illustrations were photos, my irritation was perhaps understandable.

I got busy doing more artwork and studying the new charts I had purchased. Now I had my eye on Draney Inlet, just off Rivers, and on Fish Egg Inlet a bit farther north. Winter passes quickly when you spend it making plans for summer travels. I pulled out of Vancouver in mid-June so that I'd have time to visit my friends on Cortes Island before going upcoast.

*"The Board Meeting," my painting of wooden seine boats
at Campbell River. The sports fisherman represents a hostile takeover.*

In early July I left my favourite haunt of Cortes Bay and sailed to
Campbell River to meet Margery Walker. She wanted to experience
Seymour Narrows and the Johnstone Strait area. As an added treat I
had also promised her a quick look into Knight Inlet.

Because of frightful currents in Seymour Narrows, which are
just along from Campbell River, we needed to arrive there when the
waters were ready to change direction and begin retreating upcoast.
On this day, that change occurred at 7:30 a.m. I calculated that it
would take us an hour and a half at five knots to go the distance, so
we left Campbell River in plenty of time, at 5:45. Unfortunately the
updated forecast for the day's weather was not available until six. I
had only the previous day's report, which had sounded benign.

The day before, a local fisherman had told me that the best way
to approach the narrows was to use the back-eddies up the Vancouver
Island shore. I had never tried this course before. Usually I cut across
the channel, spent the night in Gowlland Harbour, then beat my way
up the Quadra Island side, which left me fighting the current. The
fisherman's route from Campbell River pushed me along rapidly in

A gale hits at the entrance to Seymour Narrows above
Campbell River, heeling the fishboat over with the force of a gust of wind.

the desired direction. Consequently we arrived half an hour earlier
than I had anticipated. Had I known this I would have hung around
Campbell River and heard the weather report at 6 a.m., and then I
would have stayed put rather than involve us in the near disaster that
hit as we pushed through the narrows, to be greeted by the fresh
blast of a northwest gale that was building rapidly.

Because the Campbell River dock area is sheltered from much of
the strength of southeast or northwest winds, it is difficult to judge
what to expect by looking out over Discovery Passage. In our case, as
we made our way along the shore the wind was hardly noticeable
until we swung out from the shelter of the point and caught our first
view of the narrows. By then it was too late to turn back because we
would already be bucking the first of the westward tidal flow as it
streamed toward the tight passageway.

We surged out from the shelter of the point into the eddies and
riffles that were already being torn apart by blasts of wind that hurled
themselves down over the hills. A tall, slender, three-storeyed cruise
ship approached us and heeled over precariously as it struggled past

on its way downcoast. I wondered how it was going to cope with the nasty current that already threatened to slow its progress.

I worked the eddies over toward Maude Island and joined up with a few fishing boats as we all converged on the restricted passageway. I wished I'd had a chance to look at a diagram of Brown's Bay, just beyond the narrows, so we could tie up there and wait out the storm, but the pass was scattered with fishing skiffs that made navigation a hazard, so I couldn't take my eye off our course.

It quickly became apparent that we'd need the sails if we expected to make any headway in the rapidly building short, choppy waves that resulted from the outgoing current meeting the opposing wind. I turned the helm over to Margery and raised a double-reefed mainsail, all the while mentally grateful that I did not need to leave the cockpit to make any adjustment. I pulled out just enough headsail to reach as far back as the mast and soon found that we were nearly overpowered. Then all hell broke loose.

The mainsail topping lift had too much slack and looped out to catch the join in the backstay as we lurched over the sharp, short waves. I had barely freed this when the plastic replacement block holding the roller-furling line blew apart. I grabbed the tiller, put us on the other tack to give us some sea room in the narrow waterway, turned the helm back over to Margery, and dove below to my parts bin under the companionway step. I no sooner had the old metal block on and functioning than the clam cleat holding the mainsheet bent upwards so that there was no way I could secure that crucial line short of tying it off to one of the genoa cleats, which I promptly did.

Meanwhile Margery had asked for and donned a life jacket over her floater coat before grimly reaching for the tiller. I hurried to the foredeck to refasten the rubber dinghy, which chose that moment to free itself from one of the bungee cords tying it to the toe rail.

To further complicate things, the sharp waves slowed the hull down so much when we tried to tack that we had to wear away and do what we used to call a doughnut turn every time we wanted to

Union Steamship Chelosin *approaching the float in Granite Bay when this was still a very active settlement, c. 1934.*

head back across the channel. This entailed releasing the mainsheet, letting it run out, then dragging it in and retying it before I could settle down to steering past the few skiffs that remained along the edge of the waterway. I also resorted to another old racing technique of closing right into the shore before tacking because the winds there often give you a lift. Since I had fished both sides of this channel when Paul and I meandered our way along the shorelines dragging gear, I knew there was no danger near the edge, but it gave Margery regular frights as she had always employed the typical cruiser method of giving all shorelines much respect.

As the hull lurched its way along and as fresh blasts of wind occasionally heeled us right over, I grinned at Margery and reassured her that even if we lost the mast we'd still be swept along in the right direction because Granite Bay on Quadra Island was only eight miles away. Fortunately there were no more alarms. The sudden quiet when we dove behind the island that marked the passageway to our destination found us both heaving sighs of relief.

We were anchored in a nook just past the entryway to Granite Bay by 10:45 a.m., so all the excitement had only taken a few hours. We tuned in to the weather report and heard that nearby Chatham Point was experiencing gale force winds, which was not exactly news to us. Susie leaped eagerly into the dinghy and could hardly wait for a romp on shore. Had Margery been less dignified she would likely have done the same.

Like many coastal harbours, Granite Bay reveals only traces of its busy history. The cluster of pilings near the middle of the bay marks the steamer landing that served this community from the turn of the twentieth century until 1953. Around 1900 the Hastings Mills and Trading Company established one of its huge logging operations here, and the tentacles of the railway used to haul logs to Granite Bay extended in all directions right into the heart of Quadra Island. If you walk through the second-growth forest today you will still find evidence of these carefully sloped railway grades.

Of the original work force of about 500 men only Alan, a descendant of the Luoma family, remains. The Luoma brothers, Alfred and Emil, along with Emil's wife came from Finland in the early 1900s in search of land. They were farmers but the men soon found work with Hastings, which provided them with income while they struggled to establish ranches in this fertile valley. Alf's hewn-log house still stands alongside the roadway about a mile inland from Granite Bay. Unlike the usual log cabins built by pioneers, this one had logs carefully shaped with an adze so that they fit together as massive planks and needed no caulking to keep out the winter winds. The walls were smooth on both sides. Al said that it took a worker a full day to carve each log into shape, with the ends all dovetailed and locked together. Bright colour framed the many-paned windows interspersed along each side.

This sturdy house became but one of many homes in a community that boasted a school, dance hall, hotel, store, and post office, making the settlement larger than nearby Campbell River. The Coast Mission chaplain reported that the brothel was located in a floathouse moored in the bay. That place must have rocked on a Saturday night!

The staff and workers at the nearby Lucky Jim Gold Mine further enhanced the population of Granite Bay. This enterprise boasted the highest output of any B.C. mine during its heyday. The bull work of the mine was done entirely by Chinese labourers.

There was certainly little evidence of all this activity when we arrived 90 years later. Aside from the isolated cluster of pilings, an abandoned floathouse, a couple of houses on shore, and a few boats along the right-hand side we had the bay to ourselves.

After a cup of coffee and a chat with Margery about our recent hair-raising adventure, I spent the afternoon modifying the mainsheet block. The metal neck of the block had split partway across when it was bent up. I also checked out the rest of the boat gear. Weather such as we had encountered quickly shows you all the weak spots in your rigging, and I wanted no loose shackle pins or other bits of gear failure during the rest of the summer cruise. Using the radiophone, I called up my marine supply store in Vancouver and arranged for the delivery of a new mainsheet block to Port McNeill, farther upcoast, because I had no intention of spending the rest of the summer with my flimsy adaptation.

In my bunk that night I thought back over the day's adventures. Had I the opportunity to do that day over again, I would not have left shelter without a current weather report. I also thought about the gear failure. The small plastic block that had been a hand-me-over from Anne Reilly's new roller-furling equipment had obviously not been strong enough for the job I asked it to do. Its intended use was to carry the line back to the cockpit, while I liked to run my line aft, through a jam cleat, and around a turning block so that I could use my winch to help furl the headsail as I found the skinny line hard to pull in a blow. The block in question could not handle the strain of the reverse pull. It replaced an older block that had a chip out of the edge of the drum but that was metal and had served me well. Why had I tried to fix something that obviously worked?

Oh well, at least we had survived. I could certainly have used a woman from my experienced racing crew, but I had somehow managed all the emergencies, with my guest able to take over the tiller from time to time. I fell into a restless sleep, disturbed by fleeting dreams while the boat muttered now and then about the persistent gale.

We stayed put the next day, working our way into the supply of pocketbooks and studying charts that would take us to Knight Inlet. The wind continued into the third day (as so often happens on this coast), so we motored around the point into nearby Small Basin. On the way through the entrance we passed the site of a large Native summer camp, which is marked only by a grassy knoll skirted with the ubiquitous clamshells. In earlier days, before the devastation wrought by logging, Granite Bay had been crab heaven, and salmon crowded the river mouth. But logging attracted bootleggers, and liquor was far too plentiful, causing the Coast Mission minister much concern about the large seasonal influx of Natives.

Shallow, lake-like Small Inlet pleased Susie, as there was another midden beach by a streamlet on the right and an easy trail that carried you across Quadra Island to the shores of Waiatt Bay. Until recently the path to Waiatt Bay meandered through charming second-growth forest. It is now, once again, nothing but logging slash.

The wind eased in the early afternoon and we headed up Johnstone Strait. As we passed the lighthouse at Chatham Point, I noted in the log that Otter Cove, below the turn, looked like it offered good shelter from the wind that still licked the surface of the water. However, I had anchored many times on the opposite shore, behind nearby Turn Island, which had a good mud holding ground near the marshy flats, so we carried on the short distance.

The bay behind Turn Island has held many log booms in the past but I had never seen logs in the estuary by the mud flats. I reasoned that the ocean bottom here was not likely to bear too many lost boomchains, hunks of cedar bark, or other hazards to anchoring. The most recent logging company, which had almost filled the upper portion of the bay with its huge can buoys and log booms, was no longer present. We enjoyed a hike up their old road and had the place all to ourselves—and were glad of the mud bottom when the wind resumed its work that evening.

Hanging over the side of the hull was the usual onion sack containing oysters bathing in the clear water. Oysters do not thrive in the colder water beyond the various rapids that separate the Strait of Georgia from Johnstone Strait and the northern waterways, but they can tolerate a summertime dip. Since both Margery and I enjoyed eating them, I always took along a small supply. If nothing else, they are good for trading with commercial fishermen. The bag was suspended from one of the mooring cleats and hung far down below the hull. The only weakness to this arrangement is that if I forget it is there and start to move away from the anchorage, the propeller of the outboard motor invariably fouls the sack and my motor stalls. My usual response is, "Oh damn, not again!"

When it happened next morning, we were not yet out in the strong current that can run behind Turn Island, so I dropped the hook, launched the dinghy, removed the propeller, disengaged the torn sack, replaced the propeller and the cotter pin, reloaded the dinghy, started the motor, and once again hauled up the anchor. You'd think after doing all this before that I would learn. Actually that was the last time I ever got into that mess, so maybe it did some good.

The winds were quiet and we motored up Johnstone Strait. They were forecast to build again as the morning wore on, so I passed Helmcken Island on the right-hand side, which would allow us to duck into Billy Goat Bay if things got nasty. We'd had enough excitement in Seymour Narrows for one trip. Gone was the charm of the homestead established there years earlier by Mr. Hatfield. When I drew near the bay, I saw to my dismay that logging by the current owner of the island had stripped the land bare. Billy Goat Bay was now useless as shelter from winds. We forged on and, sure enough, the northwester returned. And as usual, it didn't build until we were past the underwater reef at the top of the island. Then gusts began hitting down on us. It seemed as though the high mountain on the Vancouver Island side was compressing the wind that was coming

A float camp moored in Billy Goat Bay, Helmcken Island. This bay was one of the few shelters available for small boats passing through this turbulent bit of water, c. 1950.

down the strait. We set sail and worked our way up to the shelter of the narrow inlet at Port Neville, where Margery was able to meet my friends Ole and Lily Hansen, their daughter Lorna, and her little girl.

Ole is the descendant of a family that has farmed this land for three generations. In the early years Port Neville, like Granite Bay, had experienced the boom times that come with logging. All that remained now was Ole's house, his empty log barn, and the old store-cum-post office that sits at the head of the walkway from the government wharf. Lorna built her own house here when she returned with her daughter from a failed marriage. When we visited, she was still the local postmistress and proudly stamped our letters with her official cancellation stamp.

Being stormbound had been hard on our supply of drinking water. Fortunately Ole was able to spare us some, and we carried it down to the boat in various jugs that evening. Next morning found us on our way past Robson Bight to Growler Cove. At one time a fish-buying barge and net-mending float were tied to pilings alongside the left-hand shore. My aunt often wrote about the cove when she and my Uncle Art were commercial fishing in the area. Since then the peninsula has been stripped of trees and it truly has become a "growler" cove— the wind and waves find it readily in a northwester. Nevertheless I gravitate to it because I so often see killer whales passing by.

I am not the only one to gravitate there. Whale watchers have set up a tent village above the rocky shore overlooking the strait. There is also a resident black bear that I saw by chance one evening. On that visit I arrived in the late afternoon from up north and took Susie for her run on a small peninsula that juts into the bay along the eastern shore. We made a lot of noise because the ground was decorated with bear scat, the trees had scratch marks well up their trunks, and the place smelled rank.

That evening just before dusk a handsome sailboat arrived, and soon a young mother and her two children set off for the shore to burn their garbage. They beached near my usual spot, then went off to explore before having a bonfire. Susie made a few tentative wuffs and I got a strange prickling sensation up my spine. I went out on deck with the binoculars and sure enough, there was Mr. Bear. He was loping down toward the white inflatable dinghy. I began to shout upwind to the mother to tell her to stay put. When the bear heard my voice he grabbed the garbage bag in his teeth, whirled, and crashed off through the bushes.

I kept on calling because I wasn't sure how far away the bear had gone. Meanwhile, the father heard my voice and launched his kayak to see what all the fuss was about. My concern seemed to be far greater than his, but I reasoned that this bear was unafraid of humans, what with so many whale watchers in the vicinity, and I didn't want to think of him returning for dessert.

The summer Margery and I were there we didn't see the bear. We made an early start next morning because I wanted to fish the slack tide. I was able to catch a large ling cod before we set out through Blackney Passage, and since Margery had never seen

A deserted house at Mamalilaculla with an ancient longhouse support arch beside it. The little beach house appears ready to collapse onto the clamshells.

Mamalilaculla main street, c. 1939.

Mamalilaculla we motored up Village Channel and anchored over near Grave Island. When we rowed ashore we were greeted by several Native youths who charged us five dollars each to tour the site, which they had carefully cleared with motor-driven weed-eaters. The spokesman regaled us with stories about the giant Sasquatch that he said was part of their history. I figured he'd likely been watching too much TV. I learned later that he was not even a member of that band. Perhaps that explains his ignorance of local history and legends, although one certainly had to admire his entrepreneurial spirit.

When we returned to *Juno* the sun was beating down. I draped the boat with bedding to air and we swung at anchor and enjoyed our first real warmth of the trip. Truly that village site is blessed.

With Margery's holiday time almost up, we journeyed back down Knight Inlet to Sointula on Malcolm Island to buy gifts at the gallery by the ferry dock, then motored across the pass to Port McNeill, where she caught the bus home. I put in a harbour day, did the usual chores, and prepared the boat for yet another adventure.

Passing the Cape

While studying the new chart of Smith and Boswell inlets the previous year I became fascinated by a branch of Rivers Inlet called Draney, which intruded at the upper left corner. This newly charted arm begged to be visited. Since my friend Anne Reilly had never been beyond Cape Caution, I invited her to join me for this new adventure. She would fly in to Port Hardy and I would single-hand the boat up the coast from Vancouver to meet her.

On the trip I paused at Beaver Harbour to catch a fish as a treat for her. No such luck. This was the first time I had been skunked in that area. Since I couldn't feed her fresh salmon, I took Anne out to dinner the first evening. The view from shore revealed a harbour skyline that was a blur of rigging and masts. Boats of all sizes and shapes crowded together, but they had one thing in common: they were rigged for fishing salmon, the salmon I couldn't find. With so many people in port, facilities were stretched to the limit. The inn we chose was likely at the bottom of the barrel for both supplies and energy because the meal, when it finally arrived, was a disappointment.

We left port the next morning along with the entire fishing fleet, which was heading to Smith and Rivers inlets for an upcoming fisheries

The fishing fleet waits in Port Hardy for the salmon that didn't arrive, c. 1991.

opening. (I seem to have an uncanny knack of choosing travel times when the waterways will be shrouded in nets.)

After a quiet night at anchor in Miles Inlet we set out, pushed along by a gentle southeast breeze. I didn't feel like messing around doing light-air sailing, so we powered all the way to Fury Cove in the delightful group of islands that clogs the entryway to Rivers Inlet. Well after dark, three net boats came in and anchored on one hook near the beach, where first light saw them firmly aground. Not a single head popped up. I guess their 24 hours on duty or their draining of the bottle afterwards had left them a touch indifferent. I walked Susie, hauled up the anchor, and we set out to catch our dinner.

We were not the only boats intent on the same goal. After weaving around the rocks off the entrance to Darby Channel I took one more pass in by Penrose Island and snagged a fourteen-pound spring salmon, much to the disgust of the scattered sports fishers who had no doubt paid big money for the privilege of trolling nearby. Anne couldn't resist rubbing this in and let out a few ecstatic shrieks.

These tired gillnetters never woke up when their anchored boats went aground in Fury Cove at the mouth of Rivers Inlet.

Fisheries patrol boat thunders down Darby Channel.

Net boat waiting for a fishery opening at Dawson's Landing.

Dawson's Landing was bound to have wine suitable for our anticipated feast, so we headed off up Darby Channel. This narrow passageway leads you in twists and bends past islets and bays and then through skinny gaps where your fingers can almost brush the foliage on either side. Where it opened up a bit we passed a fisheries patrol boat hurrying off in the opposite direction.

The Landing surprises you when it pops up on the left-hand side as you are about to enter Rivers Inlet. At the dock we met a pleasant young family on a net boat. When we offered them salmon steaks, the husband chuckled and instead gave us two Dungeness crab. He told us they ate any spring salmon that inadvertently got snared in their nets, and consequently they'd had their fill. He suggested we go across the inlet to Johnson Bay where we could catch more crab if we felt the urge. We did.

Since our goal was only a short distance away, we made a lazy start and cruised slowly by the old cannery site at Wadhams. I had last seen it in 1947 when I travelled on the steamship *Cardena* to work at the Goose Bay Cannery nearby. Wadhams looked to be a

The old deserted salmon cannery at Wadhams
where the grizzly was shot for being a grizzly.

lonely place with just a few buildings left standing, surrounded by berry bushes and alder trees. These factories were always placed by active flowing streams because they used prodigious amounts of water. During berry season, abandoned sites like this attract a lot of bears. During spawning season they attract eagles as well.

We were disconcerted to learn that a few days previously some Americans had gone ashore to look over the site and had disturbed a grizzly, which they subsequently shot. I'm not sure what their excuse was for being there, but I can certainly understand the bear's. The visitors said that the bear had threatened them and that they feared for their lives. Perhaps carrying a gun means that you no longer have to make lots of noise to warn the bear of your presence.

A few weeks later I talked to the loggers who worked over the hill in Draney Inlet. They said that they had never had to shoot a bear, although they were certainly surrounded by them at times. Bears love these areas because they can get at the rotten logs that are loaded with grubs and at the berries that thrive in the clearings.

After photographing Wadhams we moved on to Johnson Bay, where we nearly had our own personal bear story to tell. We motored through the outer harbour and into the area near the stream outfall. The ideal anchoring site was occupied by a fishboat, and try as I might I could not find a satisfactory alternative. A surprising amount of wind funnelled through the bay, so I elected to tie to an abandoned net float. I usually avoid these places if they appear to rely on anchors, but this one was supported by pilings and had a chain of boomsticks linking it to the shore. We tucked in behind the float, tying to the various pieces of net cord that were fastened through holes here and there. Net menders find mooring bollards a hazard for hang-ups, so you won't find standard fittings at these places.

Susie was delighted to be able to get off the boat at will until I discovered her rooting around in what appeared to be a garbage dump. It appeared that fishermen had used the almost sunken far side of the log raft as a place to attempt to burn their trash, for there were charred bacon wrappers, steak bones, and the usual doggie delights one would expect to find in such a place. Mixed in among the mess were broken bits of glass, so my dog was once again confined by the net guard that I had strung around the safety lines.

That evening I barbequed the last of our delicious spring salmon. While we relaxed over an aperitif, Anne asked if I thought a bear would ever come onto the float by walking on the logs that stretched out from the beach. I didn't want to frighten her so I scoffed at the idea. I said there were far better things for the local bears to do, what with salmon running in all the local streams. But during the night I awoke with a start when I remembered that I had left a foil-wrapped bit of cooked salmon up under the dodger to cool. If nothing else, this could attract a coon or otter. I quietly got up and tucked it into the cooler beside our dwindling supply of ice. Anne had spent the past twenty years on the night shift as head nurse, and insomnia was her middle name. The last thing I wanted was a frantically barking dog.

Next day we moved farther down the inlet to the old fishing outpost at Duncanby Landing, where we knew we could get a shower and do the laundry. Much to our delight we met the crab donor and his family. We told him we'd tied to the float in Johnson Bay.

Net boats moored stern-to at Duncanby Landing in Rivers Inlet.

"Oh, no!" he said. "Did you see the bear?"

"What bear?" I replied.

"The one that comes out onto the float to get at the garbage. We were tied up there early in the season. During the night my Lab began to whine out on the back deck so I went to see what was the matter. I caught the gleam of a bear's eyes across the float. Just then he dropped to all fours and headed for us so I cast off the lines, shoved the boat away from the dock, got the motor started, and went to drop the hook. If you are anchored with fish in the hold they've been known to swim out and try to climb aboard."

"I guess we were very, very lucky. With the sockeye running in the rivers he must have been too busy to care about garbage," I said. Anne and I talked that one over as we returned to our boat. I apologized for scoffing at her concern that night. My usual insouciance could have cost us dearly.

The breeze hit us as we stepped back on board. Southeast winds seem to march right up the passageway with enthusiasm. We later learned that the Duncanby floats have to be towed away and put into safe storage during winter gales for that reason.

It was layover time for the fishing fleet, and consequently the place was crowded. We tied on the outside because all the net boats were shoulder to shoulder along the inner edge, with many crews busy checking their nets, which stretched out across the planks and were draped over the various "horses" for easy inspection. We were no sooner settled than a huge cruiser heading along the channel in the direction of Goose Bay had us all rolling and pitching in its wake. The fishermen were incensed because the sterns of their vessels were practically touching the dock and the rollers that are used to guide the unfurling nets were vulnerable.

They told us that the previous season a humungous gin palace had roared by and completely destroyed the roller mounts on one boat. The fisherman was so angry that he leaped on board his gillnetter, accompanied by six equally cross buddies, and tore off after the offending boat. They came up behind it as it reached its destination and rammed into its swim grid. The owner hurried aft to confront them. When the fisherman demanded $750 to replace his damaged rollers, the fellow dodged behind his wife and whined, "It wasn't my fault. She was steering." He was, however, wise enough to hand over the money.

We found the outer side of the dock a restless place, but hung in there as the wind was still grumbling its way past. We did the laundry, talked to Skip Seymour, one of the current owners of the facility, and generally enjoyed watching the men at work. One evening a giant of a fisherman baited a long line, attached a five-pound lead cannonball, swirled it round and round, and flung it out into the fairway. In no time he hauled in a 40-pound halibut, which he promptly shared with all comers, including Anne and me. One visiting tourist came along to admire his catch while the fish was still hanging from his winch. When she naively asked to see the gear he had used, he posed to have his picture taken alongside the halibut, proudly displaying his fly-casting rod.

I picked the brains of both Skip and the older fishermen for information about nearby Draney Inlet. We planned to explore this waterway after I had shown Anne places like Namu and Spider Island, which is located just past the outer islands of Hakai Pass. Since I wasn't at all certain that Namu still had a store, however, we returned to Dawson's Landing to top up our food and fluid requirements.

In order to get a good start on our day we left there at 6 a.m., motored down Darby Channel, and ran smack into a fog bank that lurked near the entrance. I had spent many a day trolling this area with Paul, so we kept in sight of the shore and dragged our shallow fishing gear, but floating weeds seemed to be the only catch of the morning. When the fog lifted enough to give me confidence, we moved on toward Addenbroke lighthouse, where we planned to turn inland and explore the newly charted waterway of Fish Egg Inlet.

We entered Fish Egg behind Blair Island, pushed along by the returning southeast wind. Although we were eager to explore the area, finding good shelter for the night remained a high priority. We combed the southern shore, checking out bays and bottom texture with my fish-finding depth sounder. One spot that intrigued us was a cluster of islands, the largest just 61 metres high. They formed a lagoon with swinging room, but the sounder muttered about a rocky bottom. We reluctantly emerged through a gap in the far side, much to the annoyance of a gathering of seals that had been sunning themselves on a rock.

We moved on, watching the wind patterns and searching for a good, sheltered place to spend the night. On the large-scale chart we spotted one bay that looked promising, with a dominant M for mud. But it had a keel-cruncher of a rock barely under the water at the entrance, so I decided to have Anne hang over the bow while I ran the motor. (She was not totally comfortable handling my engine because it was somewhat different from hers on *Appleseeds*.) I told her to watch for the shallows as I edged the boat forward. Making like a figurehead, she peered down into the depths. Suddenly I saw the rock outcropping below us and abeam! I yelped and slapped the engine into reverse. She wailed in horror. I had forgotten that it takes a few years of dinghy work to learn to separate the reflections on the surface from the shadows and colours below.

We ventured into the bay but found constantly changing depths and precious little mud. I muttered a few bad words and we carried on through the narrows. I found myself longing for a power winch and at least 300 feet of line, as most useful spots were too deep to be attractive to a body that relies on muscles to haul the anchor. We made a turn past the gorgeous waterfall that empties Lois Lake, but I noticed that some of the wind seemed to be funnelling down through the gap at the head of the bay. We pressed on. The next usable niche held a large converted tug that no doubt ran a noisy electric generator. We left it to itself and headed for Fish Trap Bay. The water was deep but the wind seemed to be negligible so we dropped the hook and settled in.

Susie and I jumped into the dinghy and went off to explore the Native fish trap. It was in excellent repair except for the loss of a few rocks at the top of the wall, which had been formed with huge stones and effectively barricaded one exit from the bay between a small island and the adjacent point. The stream bed, which rounded the other side of the islet, had two longitudinal ridges built into it that would make fish netting easy as the salmon were forced to traverse the narrow channels to get to the spawning grounds. Since the tide was in, we were able to navigate one of the channels and explore the beach by the stream mouth. There was a lot of scrubby growth along the shoreline, which prevented me from finding the campground area where the families would have stayed while smoking the fish, but I could marvel at the effort and ingenuity that had been invested in the entire project.

We spent a few days sniffing out the possibilities of the area because I planned to write it up for *Pacific Yachting* that winter. As we moved on I spotted a prawn fishing boat. The prawner had just finished clearing one set of traps and was ready to move to another, so I knew he wouldn't mind an interruption. I put a ten spot into an ice-cream pail, had Anne put the boat hook through the handle, and

*This lone prawn fisherman in Fish Egg Inlet was shocked
to meet a small sailboat crewed by two middle-aged women.*

we eased alongside. The look of surprise on his face when he spotted
the two-woman crew was worth the visit. He chatted for a bit, then
threw a generous number of prawns into the bucket before moving
off. I rarely bother to set a trap myself as I am seldom in one place
for long. Also, it takes a lot of effort to pull up over 300 feet of
weighted line. I usually find that the fishermen appreciate the business.

We headed back for the entrance through Souvenir and Fairmile
passages and went up Illahie Inlet in search of Green Island Anchorage.
It was there, all shining with berry-bush foliage and ringed by
discarded clamshells indicating long-term Native use. It was indeed
a brilliantly green island, standing out from its surroundings like a
precious jewel in a handful of gravel. This was the anchorage of our
dreams: good shelter, 30 feet of depth, and mud for the hook! Out
the narrow passageway we could see what the weather had to offer in
Fitzhugh Sound, so we could decide whether to go or to stay put. We
stayed put for a second day, partly because I wanted do some artwork

My illustration for the Pacific Yachting *article about Fish Egg Inlet. The sailboat* Jammer *is anchored in front of Green Island, where longhouses once stood.*

Old-style fish packer emerges from a slit at Kwakume Inlet on its way to Prince Rupert with a load of sockeye salmon.

as I was so entranced by my surroundings, and partly waiting for the winds to ease.

The third morning we moved out between the islands and slogged along toward Namu on a rainy, windless day. The seine boats were working near the Koeye River and Kwakume Inlet. I slowed down to give Anne a glimpse. As we passed the islet-cluttered entrance to the Kwakume, a large old fish packer slipped out and headed off upcoast. I truly love the handsome lines of these wooden boats. The later aluminum workboats were built for speed and volume, not grace and charm. They seldom join my photo collection.

The heavens opened on us as we stepped off at Namu, where Kate and Al Insley greeted us at the dock. Their daughter Bev had been one of the valued members of my boat-racing team. The Insleys were on their way home from a visit to the Queen Charlotte Islands and reported that the weather had been fabulous. We seemed to be more like the doleful cartoon character that is perpetually under a rain cloud. We'd even brought it to Namu.

There was more disappointment at Namu. BC Packers had sold the whole kit and caboodle to three partners who were trying to hold it together with wrapping paper and string. The floats had always been loosely fastened, as they had to be hauled away each winter. (To the local Natives, "namu" means hurricane. You couldn't leave anything in that open bay in the off-season.) Now the sections were tied together with odd bits of rope. The small seasonal village that I had known years ago when I came here with Paul was no more. At that time it had been totally committed to maintaining and supplying fishing boats, canning salmon, and housing the workers. Now, almost all the services had either been moved into the grocery store or had ceased to exist. The store itself was abysmally stocked and staffed. There was no question that the new partners had bitten off more than they could chew, and what they had bitten off was a pile of decrepit buildings and a dying business. It never ceases to amaze me that original owners can sell out and walk away, leaving a blight on the landscape.

Seine boats fill outer floats at Namu while fish packers anchor in the bay to haul the catch away to canneries. Namu cannery, by 1990, functioned only as a fuel, icing, and transfer depot.

Fishermen struggle with a reluctant splice on their seine boat at Namu.

The derelict Namu "Hilton" was home to a huge cannery work force in earlier days.

What was left, we used gratefully: the fuel service, the tiny hamburger joint, and the hilarious showers where you were glad you had remembered your rubber thongs but found yourself wishing there was a door lock as the facilities were open to all passers-by. Sometimes you even heard loud male voices because the outer room housed the washtubs used by both sexes.

Most cruisers today boast hot running water, showers, and sometimes even onboard laundries, but ours had none of these. Living on a 25-foot sailboat is akin to camping out in the wilderness. We tended to gravitate toward places that offered showers and, oh joy, a laundromat. Betweentimes we resorted to basin baths and a generous supply of fresh underwear. Saltwater soap and a sturdy swimming ladder are alternatives, but not up north where the water is positively glacial. One thing I have learned is to hang all wet towels and facecloths out under the awning so that the bedding stays dry. Moisture inside the cabin is an open invitation to mildew.

Rain pelted down as we left for Nalau Passage on our way to Spider Island. I had always been attracted to Spider Island because it had not only been a war-time military base serving a gun emplacement, but had also survived for years afterwards as an offloading port for the fishing industry. Growing up in the war years I could remember hearing the groans from servicemen who had been assigned to that remote spot, and I had heard fishing uncles and cousins speak of it as well. Unbeknown to me, it had totally reverted to wilderness. Nevertheless Anne and I were Spider-bound.

En route we tucked into a bay on the sheltered side of Underhill Island as the southeast winds had returned and were expected to get worse. Anne was delighted with the shelter

Anne watches me row Susie ashore for a pit stop near the tiny anchorage in Nalau Passage.

offered by the inlet, and Susie figured the beach would do after having been confined to the leash at Namu.

The wind was no worse in the morning, so we moved out of Nalau Passage into Kildidt Sound through the southeast swells to the passage by Manley Island. My old charts still had my compass headings penciled onto them and I had determined the Loran waypoints, so we set off across the open stretch. I am always conscious of current when I cross this waterway as there are impressive reefs to the left and the little green bumps on the horizon give no indication of where you will find the pass. But find it we did. To traverse it you have to squiggle your way past myriad islets and make abrupt right-angle turns through narrow gaps. When I told an old fisherman about the route I preferred, he chuckled and told me I had found the "back door." The front door, through Brydon Channel, looked undoable as far as I was concerned, loaded as it was with rock outcroppings.

Because dirty weather was building again, I anchored in the secure haven at the lower end of Hurricane Island, hoping that it was a misnomer. When I studied the charts with Anne we found many wartime labels such as Spitfire Channel, Kittyhawk Group, and Lancaster Rocks. The airmen had left their mark here, as had the navy at Fish Egg with labels such as Fairmile, Patrol, and Convoy passages. So it was likely that Hurricane had nothing to do with weather.

Since Namu had hardly been the supermarket of the north and since we were tired of eating out of tins, we went fishing for rock cod, which were only too glad to nibble our offerings. The beaches were non-existent. I wished that we could have anchored in the prettier site between Edna and Anne islands, but that had to wait for the next day after the weather settled a bit.

Sure enough, when I moved us to that lovely area we got one day of calm and then the winds increased. I slid the kellet down the anchor line after letting out more scope. The kellet, in my case, was a ten-pound fishing cannonball clipped onto a snatch block and restrained by a length of line. By running it about halfway down my anchor line, the angle of pull on the chain and anchor was lowered considerably. This also drew my boat more out of the swells. However, Anne slept poorly, so Susie and I went out foraging alone at low tide next morning.

This area had been abalone heaven at one time, but since the floating sport-fishing camps had arrived and since abalone fishing had attracted commercial interest, there were none to be found. There was already a ban on harvesting them, for good reason, so I settled for a couple of sea cucumbers and a pair of seven-inch sea urchins. I suspect that harvesting these is also banned by now.

I stripped the muscles from the sea cucumber and put them on ice for next day, but tonight was sushi night. I kept the ingredients

Susie inspects large sea urchins. The roe is much prized for making sushi.

for this delicacy on board. Perishables like long English cucumber were not always available, but the dried seaweed wrapping (nori), powdered horseradish (wasabi), and sticky rice kept well, along with canned smoked eels and my own smoked salmon. If I had fresh salmon, red snapper, geoduck, or sea-urchin roe it was gourmet heaven. I stripped the mandarin-orange-shaped segments of roe from the sea urchin and nestled them on top of rice balls wrapped in a collar of nori. With the saki jug warming in a pot of water, we were in for a treat.

The weather remained awful and the liquor cabinet was dry so we up-anchored during the first lull and headed back to Fury Cove, then left for Dawson's Landing the next morning. The accident that happened on our arrival there changed everything.

With *Saffron*, it had become my practice, when we came down a narrow slot and had to make a sharp turn and land on the off-side of the dock, to have one crew member stand at the shrouds and step onto the tip of the float with the bowline in hand, then hurry along in case the nose of the boat contacted the main walkway. Currents were invariably bad and the dock finger was short, so there was no way that person could step off at the cockpit and still do their job. Out of habit, I retained this practice when docking anywhere. This proved to be Anne's undoing.

When we approached Dawson's fuelling station, Anne had to climb outside the netting I had strung on the life lines to keep Susie on board. Anne stood on the toe rail with her boot-tips and clung to the shrouds with one hand while holding the bowline in the other. As she turned to step off the boat she caught her boot in the netting and clung to the boat with her other foot already on the dock. The boat was still moving forward in the brisk current as I had not turned the throttle far enough to completely stop the hull. (I should have docked against the flow but there was a hull in the way.) I heard a shriek and saw her collapse onto the float.

She was in terrible pain and began throwing up, so there was no doubt that she had broken a bone in her arm. I applied a sling, got her back on board, finished the fuelling, moved the boat around out of the way, tied Susie on a long line, and then tried to get Anne into a comfortable position while I figured out what to do. Bob Bachen, at the store, told me that Medevac would come in with a helicopter and evacuate her to Port Hardy, but Anne would have none of this. She was sure she'd be better in the morning and we could go on with our plan to explore Draney Inlet together. However, after putting in a miserable night half-reclining on the settee among a pile of cushions, she agreed that she needed medical help.

The helicopter showed up by midmorning, but the first-aid attendant could not give Anne any medication to ease the pain, as it would interfere with the diagnosis at the hospital. She had looked forward to seeing Cape Caution and all the islands in Queen Charlotte Sound from the air, but instead spent her time crouched over a barf bag. Since she was a registered nurse who had put in many years as head night nurse at the hospital in Richmond and had attended more broken bones than she cared to remember, she knew exactly what was the matter, but that cut no ice with either the doctor on call (it was a Sunday) nor the X-ray technician, who had to leave a family picnic to read the results. They both scoffed at her; she was refused adequate painkillers and told to fly away home.

Her son Chris, who was a skilled orthopaedic surgeon, took one look at the X-ray she brought down with her and said, "Well, Mom, you cracked the top of your humerus. No wonder you're sporting such an ugly black bruise."

As for myself, I watched the helicopter leave, went back on board, and sat there stunned. What was I going to do? Somehow Cape Caution had always been the cutoff point for my solo coastal travel. I never once envisioned that I could be north of it, alone. The old feelings of inadequacy oozed to the surface, just as they had when I found myself in Barkley Sound with no one available to help me take the boat back to Vancouver.

Fleeting horrors clouded my vision. I knew of no one who would come and help me get the boat back to civilization. What was I going to do? Then Susie came and laid her muzzle on my knee. She knew that I was troubled. I rubbed her ears, thanked her, then went below and hauled out the charts and my dividers. I found to my surprise that there was no crossing longer than fifteen miles from shelter to shelter to get me back to Port Hardy, and I'd been that far north alone before. What was there to be afraid of? As for Draney Inlet, what was the big deal? I had the new chart and I had Susie for company. It was time to get on with my adventure.

In the afternoon I motored to Taylor Bay on Walbran Island because it offered good shelter and was right across from the entrance to Draney Inlet. The bay was delightful, dotted with tiny moss-covered islets and a fine view across the channel. We climbed into the dinghy before supper and rowed over to explore a beach where there was a solitary leaning piling. Beyond it was a meadow all aglow in the late afternoon sun. As we followed a pathway up from the beach I thought that we had found a deserted homestead, but, no, it was a graveyard. What a surprise in such an out-of-the-way place! Then I remembered that this area, along with much of the B.C. coast, had been occupied by settlers and handloggers as well as seasonal cannery workers. The floating missionaries had been as active here as they were around the lower coast.

I finally understood the term "pushing up daisies" as we moved among the shoulder-high flowers with stems thicker than my finger. One white cross caught my attention. It read MARY AMANDA PERRY, which sounded more like someone from *Gone With the Wind* than Rivers Inlet. Wanting to learn more about this lady with the gentle-sounding name, I made a mental note of her dates and headed back to the boat and supper. I'd return in the morning with the camera.

We woke to fog—so thick I couldn't even see the bow of the boat. By now I was all geared up to make my foray into Draney Inlet and chafed at the delay. After breakfast and a damp walk with Susie on the nearest islet, I noticed that the fog was thinning. I got out my chart and tide tables and made some calculations. It wasn't much of a run straight across to the entrance. If I neared the shore up-inlet from the narrows, I could slide in along the left-hand side at slack water and tuck into the bay around the corner. There appeared to be no rocks along that shore, so I should be safe enough.

I needed to get to Draney at change of current, so I set out in good time. When I neared what should have been the entrance, all I found were swarms of sport-fishing skiffs from the nearby fishing lodge. It would be nearly impossible to pick my way through them, what with their trailing lines, so I veered off to the right and bounced down the side of the channel to Duncanby Landing. There was no sign of wind so I could come close to the shore, then ease off, watching my sounder all the while. Having grown up before the days of radar I did not feel deprived, only cautious.

I also felt that I could just as well have stayed put and gotten my picture of the graveyard. As it happened, when I wrote up Draney Inlet later for *Pacific Yachting*, I made an error in Mary Amanda's dates and was gently chastized by a woman who had paddled the coast all the way to Alaska, visited Mary by canoe, and found her very much alive when I said she was gone.

At Duncanby Landing, Skip Seymour filled me in on some of Mary Amanda Perry's story. I got the rest of it from Mimi Hayes, who wrote to me after the article was published. Mimi and her husband had spent a couple of years at Rivers Inlet in the late 1950s while he was a fisheries officer based at Dawson's Landing.

Mimi reported that Mrs. Perry had come to the area as cook at a floating logging camp and had elected to stay on when the camp's owners went broke and left. In lieu of pay, she inherited the camp. Mimi writes about her first visit to Mrs. Perry's floating home: "We had tea and admired her bountiful garden on shore as well as the dinner-plate-sized begonias hanging from the window boxes of her home! Her tomatoes must have inspired the story *The Revenge of the Killer Tomatoes*. They were humungous. Tomatoes and begonias grew from a starfish buried at the bottom of each hole. The vast cabbages etc. no doubt had plenty of fish and seaweed to nourish them. Quite a feat in an area where the soil is sour in the extreme and the rainfall measures about 240 inches a year."

Mimi says that in her youthful naiveté she enquired about Mr. Perry. Apparently they had lived at a mining town in South America and, Mrs. Perry reported, "He fell down a mine shaft and got killed; served him right, the dirty bugger." Mrs. Perry finished raising her family alone, mostly at the camp in Draney Inlet. To quote Mimi, "She was not your average Mrs. Canadian housewife! She was reputed to be able to shoot the eye out of a no-see-um at 50 feet. She had suffered a bad jolt or kick-back from a 10 gauge shotgun while attempting to scare a bear out of her garden and now had the big gun erected on a tripod with a long cord attached to the trigger. She quite rightly feared bears.

"Regularly, every [we'll say] Tuesday at 10 a.m. would appear Axel Johnson who lived at Allard Bay at the other end of Draney. This caused much merriment, as in this isolated spot where only friends, food and fish were of import—who cared for timetables and exactitudes? We didn't understand at first that this was a safety factor, and indeed one fateful morning Axel did not show up. Mrs.

Perry hastened as fast as she could row in her skiff to Axel's to find him near death from mauling by a grizzly. She rowed him all the way to Wadhams and saved his life."

In her letter, Mimi goes on to say, "Axel hunted and bucked wood [for their stoves] Mrs. Perry canned, gardened and baked. She had a screened hanging closet in which a mowich [deer] usually hung in an airy breezeway between the buildings. I think Axel was the recipient of a lot of her cooking and baking, too.

"In 1957, the crew of the *Egret Plume II* [the fisheries patrol boat] including Dave [Mimi's husband], the minister and skipper of the United Church Mission boat *Thomas Crosby IV*, a Reverend Howard, and his crew of able bodied men, added a sixth tier of new floater logs under Mrs. Perry's outfit. This was an every ten year event." (These logs became so riddled by teredos, a marine wood-borer, that they became virtual sponges in a matter of years.)

Now I knew it was the United Church Mission that had cared for the graveyard on Walbran Island. Mimi said that they had to cover the graves with more soil every few years because it was so sparse and the rainfall was so awesome. And one can only be amazed at Mrs. Perry's determination to stay in such a hostile environment, but obviously she had it tamed to her liking. Certainly the Draney Inlet I saw during that sunny visit was a place of tranquil beauty. The channels were wide and the hills sloped back so you didn't feel the claustrophobia of some of the passageways in coastal waters.

Susie and I traversed the narrows and entered Draney Inlet one morning in early August. The logging operation in the bay to the left was already halfway through its day's work. In summer they go from dawn to early afternoon, using dew to reduce the fire hazard. There was a floating A-frame that lifted the medium-sized second-growth logs clear of the slope and hurried them down into the water with minimal damage to the terrain. The usual whistle toots and rumbles filled the air. I snapped a few pictures and ambled on my way. I wanted to get right to the end of the inlet and spend the night there.

The afternoon northwesterly gave us a slow run that petered out past Robert Arm. The breeze seemed to have gone there to inspect the clearcut that had stripped the hills, leaving them bare and ugly. (This must have been the work of the large camp in neighbouring Boswell Inlet.) With not enough air to move the boat, I rolled up the sails and started the motor. When I came to the dogleg by Allard Arm where Axel had lived, it appeared to be good crab-pot country, but I reasoned that it also looked like bear country because of the spawning streams. If I anchored there I would have to go ashore with the dog, and my deafness leaves me feeling a tad cautious where bears are concerned. We moved on.

It was pure delight on that sunny day to be moving in waters I had never before explored, all by myself except for Susie. But the delight didn't last. Halfway down the new passageway I was literally bombarded by monster horseflies that bit clear through my shirt. I flailed around with the fly swatter, stopping every so often to sweep up the carcasses because Susie found them delicious. In the midst of this mayhem I spotted the glistening waterfalls fanning out of Caroline Lake.

I was dumbstruck. Really dumb, because I also nearly clipped an exposed rock pinnacle that appeared to port. It was on the chart but I had been too preoccupied to keep it in mind. When I thought this one over I realized that I had seen it because my guardian spirit had asked me to glance about at the right moment and I had obeyed the command. Just beyond this exposed rock is one that is hidden—a handy arrangement for nervous navigators.

At the bend near the waterfall I found islets and small bays with enchanting views in all directions. I also found more horseflies than I care to remember. When I talked later to Skip Seymour about this phenomenon he said that it is seasonal. Had I been there a few weeks later or earlier I probably wouldn't have found any horseflies. As it was, they nearly drove Susie and me to distraction. I took soundings, eyeballed possible anchoring spots, and used the fly whacker. Then I pulled out into the passageway, left the boat drifting, took Susie indoors, installed my canvas door panel, and sat down to figure out what to do. If I stayed

A painting of the Draney Inlet sunrise with Juno *superimposed on the scene. Mary Amanda Perry's old float houses were to the left of the picture, and the logging camp is on the right near Fishhook Bay.*

I'd have to remain indoors till dusk, when horseflies gave way to blackflies, closely followed by the nightly scourge of mosquitoes. These fellows certainly had invented the whole time-share idea.

There was no way I wanted to remain indoors on such a hot day. Down below in a sailboat, you might as well be in a dungeon; you can see nothing unless you stand up and peer out the slits of windows. I made some lunch, sat, and thought some more. Life on board a sailboat had suddenly become almost unbearable. I wanted screens and windows and cross-ventilation. I wanted to be able to spend a day like this with my sketchbook and my paints. Here I was, surrounded by breathtaking scenery, and I couldn't see it. There had to be a better way to enjoy this coast.

There was nothing for it but to leave the horseflies to the deer and bears and go back to anchor near the entryway. (Generally these pests favour the heads of inlets and are rare on the outer coast.) I got out the camera, took some photos, fired up the outboard, and retraced my path. The wind near Robert Arm had us tacking the length of the inlet, but it was cooler that way. I dropped the anchor in Fishhook Bay and Susie enjoyed a much-delayed afternoon walk.

She woke me at the first glimmer next morning. I went out to discover what had disturbed her and saw the fast "crummy" from the floating logging camp just before it disappeared behind the point. I set up my old Pentax camera on the stern railing with the shutter speed slowed right down so I could capture that first delicate glow in the distance. I took two more photos, each fifteen minutes apart, as the colour brightened. The wake of the boat finally reached us in the last photo, the only ripples to distort the mirror image of dawn.

I spent the early morning emptying the crab pot and rambling the beach with Susie until I saw smoke emerge from the cookhouse at the floating camp. Now was the right time for a visit. No doubt the cook had been up by three to prepare breakfast and would have taken a short rest before getting on with the baking.

The camp was a trip down memory lane—shades of Teakerne Arm in the 1930s, with pock-marked, unpainted wooden floors. The bunkhouses and the machine shop were all laced together and resting on massive logs. Coffee and cookies awaited me in the cookhouse as Irene, the cook, had seen me coming. She told me that Mrs. Perry had raised a large family here, but someone named Debotte now lived at her place, which was anchored right next door. She didn't know if they were relations. The huge KEEP OUT signs certainly did not reflect Mary Amanda Perry's style of hospitality. But then Mary represented a different time on this coast, when none of us had a key to our door.

I left Draney in the last half-hour of an ebb tide and kept to starboard as there was a huge back-eddy ripping up the other side of the channel. My sailboat shot out of the narrows like a cork out of a bottle, causing the sport fishers to look up in astonishment. I was a tad surprised myself.

We motored back to Duncanby to write up what I had learned and to wait out the latest gillnet fishery. I was unwilling to do the Cape Caution leg alone through tangles of salmon nets.

Dozer boat pulls around in front of the cookhouse in Draney Inlet.

I finally left early on a cold, damp morning. Swarms of sport-fishing boats crowded the shoreline near the south entrance to Rivers Inlet. I was shivering my way down toward Egg Island when the snuggery between Ann and Table islands called me in. I decided to take a shortcut and go through the Cluster Reefs instead of taking the long course down Loran Passage. Weaving my way through the massive kelp beds that crowd the mouth of Smith, I kept my eye on the sounder and watched for shallows. The chart indicated 23 feet at datum on the highest underwater peak, but the usual swells made me nervous. Nothing untoward happened, so I cut my way past Ann Island and dropped the anchor just behind the northern point of Table Island.

Once the hook was well set I went below and made a cup of tea. Cupping my hands around it for warmth, I sat in the cockpit under the dodger and waited to see how the hull would react to my choice of anchorage. Pacific swells rumbled on the outside of the islands, but the boat simply rolled gently with its nose into the breeze coming

The last net boat backs away from this packer at Table Island, signalling the end of the fishery for that season.

through the gap. One fish packer remained in the harbour, unloading the last boat. Since the packer didn't leave right away, I rowed over for a visit and to see if they could spare me a bit of ice. In exchange, they asked if I had any extra salt as they were fresh out and wanted to can some salmon. A crew member came over to *Juno* a bit later for the salt and brought me a nice sockeye fillet. With food to eat and ice to keep it cool I would be able to stay in Smith for a few more days.

Low tide encouraged us to do a beach ramble, so Susie and I went to explore the chain of islets that almost bind the large islands together. We could stand and look out over the ocean with nothing between us and Japan but the curvature of the earth. What a glorious thought!

Swept by the waves into pockets of gravel were empty mussel shells as long as my hand, typical of this area. When I had tried eating these large models in the past the toughness and the brilliant orange flesh put me off, but the iridescence of their interior, all puddled with salt water reflecting trees and clouds, kept me moving from one to the next.

The big and small of the mussel family. The large one is as long as a hand.

Susie wuffed and I turned to see what had attracted her attention. Seals were humping their way around the top of an exposed reef, moving from right to left in their effort to elude a large killer whale that was trying to snag them as the swells nearly lifted him over the weed-shrouded outcropping. I watched, fascinated. After a while the orca tired of the game and moved off after easier prey. One old seal in the water between the reefs gave Susie and me a worried look before he lifted his chin and slid backwards under the surface. The others on the reef relaxed, so we went on with our ramble.

The soil, where there was any, was rich and mixed with fragments of shells, making me think that the Native people must have come here to spear ling cod in season. The large male cod guards the cluster of eggs until they hatch, so he is easy prey. Ann Island is classified as Indian reserve, so at one time it fell within the harvesting territory of a band.

The large islands were quite different in structure. Ann Island was the usual rocky outcropping, while Table was all upward thrusting plates and flat on top, wearing a brushcut of straggly trees. Eagles,

Juno *anchored at the mouth of Smith Sound, with Table Island's upthrusting rock formation visible on the right. The eagle's nest is out of sight on a bare tree at the top. (Japan is behind you in this scene.)*

with their usual disregard for the comfort of their babies, had built their nests high in a snag near the gap in the islands. I suppose it was the best place to eyeball any dinner rising from the ocean's depths, like window-shopping while you baby-sat, but the rain and wind would have been a corker to endure.

On our way back to the boat I rowed through a sickly looking scabrous forest, all that remained of a field of bull kelp. The heads had been stripped of their fronds. At first I thought this must have been the work of herring-roe harvesters and wondered why they didn't leave one leaf per bulb so that small creatures would have a place to browse. I supposed this would cut too deeply into the profits. The good side of this type of roe gathering is that the fish live to spawn for many more years. But then I thought that maybe I was fussing about nothing and that all the damage had come from propellers raking away at the kelp while net fishermen waited to unload at the packers that moored here in season. I did not know the answer to that puzzle.

We returned to the boat to find the fish packer gone. It was late in the day and the evening sun dappled the low hills that form Smith Sound, making this anchorage a place of beauty. I thought we had the bay to ourselves but as I turned to go below I spotted three humpback whales feeding along the outer edge of the kelp bed. They were huge creatures, much larger than *Juno*, but I felt no threat as they went quietly about their business nearby. Susie was completely mesmerized by their presence.

I no sooner sat down to supper than Susie told me we had more company. A medium-sized aluminum dive boat towing a large black inflatable had come into the bay and was setting its anchor nearby. Drat. I had hoped to have this special place to myself. After a while six young people climbed into the rubber boat and came alongside to tell me that they were planning a beach barbeque. Did I want to join them? Since I was already eating I told them I would come along later. So much for my desire to be alone.

They built a roaring fire on the beach on Ann Island and were soon cooking salmon and enjoying their beer. I rowed Susie ashore and we had a visit. They were scuba divers and had been exploring all the old cannery sites of the midcoast. A slightly older fellow seemed to be the skipper, and he asked us all if we'd like to go whale watching. None of us was wearing a life jacket for our beach outing, and a visit to the whales seemed harmless enough, so we all got into the inflatable with its huge engine and zoomed off out of the harbour.

Judging by the initial boat handling I should have asked then and there to be left behind, but I said nothing. When the fellow running the boat spotted a dark shining hump rising out of the water, he roared over to the exact spot where the whale sounded and cut the motor. Each time the behemoth came up for air he repeated the move. We all began to protest that he was harassing the whale, but he laughed and called us "chicken." If I hadn't been clutching my dog I'd have "chickened" him, but I was afraid to loosen my grip because she nearly jumped out of the boat each time that great back rose from the water. In a matter of seconds the whale's nostrils opened, exhaled, drew in air, shut with a sigh, and then the water closed over them. In a silken swirl the whale went back down to feed. I couldn't help wondering how it managed all this in storm conditions, with the nose right on top amid the crashing waves.

Over and over again we dashed from spot to spot until the whale got fed up and sounded in deeper water. I am still amazed at how patient this huge creature was with the meanness of the helmsman. During the night the whales came in again near my boat, huffing and snuffling. Susie muttered about their presence and my nose told me they were there. When I awoke next morning I was glad to find the scuba boat gone.

I finally had Smith all to myself. During this trip I had become intrigued by the many small, tree-encrusted islets of the midcoast. Wind had sculpted the growth into wild shapes that gave each a distinctive appearance, so I set off with the camera ready and worked my way into the inlet. Before long I spotted salmon jumping and began to drag a lure as well. This presented a challenge because invariably the rod would bend with a strike as I lined up another great shot. The dilemma was solved when I lost my lure on a rock outcropping, but I had three small pink salmon in the cockpit by then, as well as a handful of good snaps, so I cleaned up the mess and headed for the unglamorously named Fly Basin.

Since pink salmon do not keep well there was nothing for it but to get out the pressure cooker and do some canning. I put the offal in a crab pot, but soon discovered that the fishermen had dined on crab all summer and only babies and females were left. I released them and went off to explore with Susie. The bay is not inspirational, surrounded as it is with like-sized trees and no hills or view at all. What it does have is a good mud bottom and room for a lot of boats.

The marine weather report forecast another southeast wind but promised that it would be weak. I began building up some anxiety about rounding Cape Caution again. When I checked out the breeze in the morning it seemed manageable, and I reasoned that I could always duck back into Jones Cove if I didn't like the way things were going. So off we went.

When I reached Egg Island I turned to look at the Cape and saw whale spume backlit by the morning sun. The family was languidly feeding in the shallows and, as usual, the presence of sea creatures comforted me. I was also relieved to find that the wind was steadily veering around to the southwest, so the front was already passing. It was a cinch to unfurl the genoa as the main was already up and pulling, so I cut the motor and turned to reach down the coast to Miles Inlet. It became a vigorous sail because the wind defied my analysis and built to about twelve knots. I burst forth into song. *Juno* was hardly the Wabash Cannonball, but she didn't seem to care as the hull chuckled and the tiller vibrated under my hand. It was a happy boat to be back doing what it was built to do. And I was a joyful skipper sailing alone past an imagined hazard in my precious craft.

I made the turn at Harris Island and we scorched our way down the narrow passageway into the anchorage. I furled the headsail, put on the automatic pilot, and went forward to prepare the anchor. When we neared the junction of the waterways I unhooked the pilot, released the mainsheet, then went forward and lowered the anchor, tied off the line, and waited for the hull to nose into the wind when the hook grabbed the mud. After tidying up the boat and walking Susie, I settled down in the shelter of the dodger with a gin and tonic.

A feeling of great satisfaction came over me. At 64 years of age I had finally conquered an impressive obstacle in my coastwise cruising. And the goals I had set years ago at the behest of Rollo Boas were no longer a remote vision; they were a fact. I had wanted to learn to handle my boat well, to develop as an artist, and to become a writer. The last of the four goals was elusive, but Susie was doing her best to fill that void.

*June and Susie stand on the otter playground in
Miles Inlet, with* Juno *securely anchored in the gap.*

From all this I have learned that each time you accept a challenge
and master it, the next one seems less of a threat, so that life opens
up in front of you as a series of capes to be rounded, each one leading
you to shelter from the storm. The passing of each cape in my life
has brought with it a great sense of happiness and fulfillment. And as
long as I keep setting new goals for myself, life will go on and be lived
with vigour.

Glossary of Sailing Terms
According to June

abeam: To one side

aft: Near the stern

amidships: In the middle of the ship

back deck: As opposed to the foredeck

backstay: Cable that supports the mast from aft

backwind: Wind coming on the wrong side of the sail

barging: In a race, an illegal move at the start line in which a boat tries to squeeze in where no room exists

beam reach: Sailing with the wind coming broadside to the hull

beam sea: Waves approaching broadside to the hull

beat, or beating to weather: The act of sailing into the wind, zigzagging upwind

boom: A metal pole attached to the mast to which the lower edge of the mainsail is attached

boom-vang: A set of two pulleys and a line that are used to hold the boom down

bosun's chair: A canvas seat used to hoist a crew member up the mast

bow: Forward end of a boat

bow line: The line used to tie the boat's bow to the dock

bow pulpit: A metal railing at the boat's bow

broach: A nearly out-of-control situation where the boat turns broadside to the wind

catabatic wind: A venturi effect where the wind slides down a valley and out to sea clam cleat: A mechanical device used for grabbing and holding a line

close-hauled: Sailing as close into the wind direction as possible

cockpit: The part of the boat where the helmsperson and crew stand

cockpit drains: Openings to drain water out of the cockpit

committee boat: In a race, the anchored boat that is staffed by the race committee and that marks the right-hand end of the starting line

commodore: An elected official, the chairperson of a yacht club

companionway: The passageway down into a boat's cabin

corrected time: Each boat has an ideal speed. In a race, the amount of time actually elapsed is compared to the boat's ideal speed. Corrected time is the result of this arithmetic calculation.

dodger: Much like a baby-carriage hood, the dodger protects the companionway from driven spray and rain

douse the sail: Lower and bundle a sail

drifter: A very lightweight sail for use in near windless conditions

echo sounder: A sonar device that echoes a signal off the ocean bottom to indicate depth of water

fender: A rubber bumper put between the hull and a dock

floating stern line: A length of floating line used to keep an anchored boat from rotating over a rock or shoal. This line is usually brightly coloured to ensure its visibility.

foresail: Any sail fastened to the bow of the boat

forestay: A cable between the bow of the boat and the top of the mast to provide forward support for the mast

furling drum: A drum at the base of the roller-furling system on which a control line is wound

genoa: A large-size foresail

GPS (Global Positioning System): A satellite-reflecting electronic device that indicates your position on the earth's surface

halyard: A line used to haul a sail up the mast

head: Marine toilet

headsail: A sail that is forward of the mast, for example, the genoa

helm: The steering device, either a tiller or a wheel. "At the helm" means to be in control.

hull: The body of a boat

jib: A small genoa

jibe: To bring the boat around to the other tack when sailing with the wind

keel: In sailboats, this is a weighted fin fastened to the bottom of the boat

kellet: A weight that is run partway down the anchor line to alter the angle of pull

lazarette: A storage bin, usually aft on a boat

leeward: On the off-wind side

life line: A safety line running the length of the deck; a body harness can be clipped onto it so if a person goes overboard, he or she is still attached to the boat

Loran (*long-range navigation* system): A navigational device that determines position based on radio signals emanating from fixed positions on land

luffing: Coming head-on into the wind; this is one way to slow down while under sail

mainsail: The sail fastened to the mast and to the boom

mark boat: A boat used to mark a turning point in a race

mark roundings: Going around a mark on the race course (These marks are usually anchored temporarily)

mast: The upright metal or wooden post on a boat

masthead: The top of the mast

monohull: A boat with a single hull, as opposed to a multihull

multihull: A boat with two or more hulls joined together to provide stability

outboard: Usually refers to a small motor fastened outside the hull

poled: A pole can be temporarily hooked to one corner of the genoa to hold the bottom of the sail away from the boat

port: Left-hand side of the boat

quarter the waves: To go diagonally over the crest of a wave so that the hull does not pound

reach: A point of sail between close-hauled and running

reef-in: A way to reduce the working area of a sail

right of way: A boat to your right has right of way, as does one with the wind coming over the starboard rail

roller-furling: A form of reefing in which the sail, for example, a headsail, can be mechanically rolled around the headstay to reduce the amount of cloth exposed to the wind

running before: To sail with the wind rather than against it

Sabot: The brand name of a one-person small sailboat

safety harness: A body harness used to fasten a person to a boat

sailpast: A formal parade of boats to salute the commodore of a yacht club

sheave: The moving part of a pulley that guides the line

sheets: Lines tied to a sail

shortened sail: A reefed sail

spinnaker: The large pigeon-breasted sail used when running before the wind

stem: The support area at the very front end of the hull, as in the bow stem

stern: The back or aft end of a boat

stern-tied: Tied at the stern

storm jib: A small, heavy-duty sail used in very strong winds

tack: Heading off in the other direction to the flow of the wind

tiller: A wooden bar used to turn the rudder

toe rail: A ridge around the edge of the deck

topping lift: A line that gives support to the aft end of the boom

trailing edge: The "back" edge of a sail

turning vessel: The anchored boat that marks a turn in a race course

tying a reef: A reefed mainsail usually has ties that hold the bottom edge down to the boom

venturi wind: A wind that speeds up as it is squeezed between land forms

whisker pole: A light, portable pole used to hold the trailing corner of a headsail away from the hull when running before the wind

windward: Toward the direction of the wind flow

Photo Credits

Front cover: *Saffron* beating to weather. June near Cape Scott (inset). Back cover: Slipping through the gap by the Southgate Group of Islands, bound for Allison Harbour (top). Susie inspecting a large sea urchin (middle). June painting on board the *Juno* tied up at the wharf in Cortes Bay (bottom).

Acknowledgements

I could not have done the things I did while learning to sail, race, and cruise my boat without the enthusiastic help of a number of men. This is partly because, at that time, few women were skilled electricians, shipwrights, or mechanics. When mechanical things went wrong it was men who came to my rescue. Years ago, before his untimely death, I was informed by my dear neighbour Chris Conti that all angels are male. But when I have been in trouble at sea and called on my own private sea god, I have always referred to a female deity. She helped bolster my confidence and lead me to choose the right path. So I can say with some conviction that all my rescuers have been celestial.

And I have learned from my angels. It seems that when a need arose, they were there. Perhaps it is as Robert Fulghum says, "When the pupil is ready the teacher appears." Had anyone offered advice before I needed it, I would not have been able to incorporate that knowledge into my being.

Although males helped during the learning curve, it was females who did the grunt work of actual boat handling. My racing crew was made up of capable, brave young women who endured wet, cold, and storm, enthusiastically showing up at the boat, obeying all orders, and accepting our share of losses. I tried to make it fun and never chastized them for mistakes because I made my share too. Some already knew more than I did when they joined the crew and some were simply people who loved being on the water. As much as possible, I had the beginners learn to handle all positions and encouraged them to use the boat when I was not available. Many went on to own boats themselves, and if they didn't own one they were welcome as crew members elsewhere.

Aside from Michelle James, who was always with me, my most active racing crew members included Eleanor Frisk, Diane Fast, Wendy Grider, Sharleen Griffin, and Aldyen Donnelly. Others who came when they could were Peri Mehling, Sue Barton, Charlene Lefeaux, Bev Insley, Rosemary Anderson, Sally Davies, Trudy Cameron, Marion Vanderwood, Meg Hill, Karen Renfrew, Phylis Lauriente, and Carol Cardew. My two sailboats would not have earned all the honours they did without these brave young women. A boat is only as good as its crew, and these people were magnificent. They left me with memories to last a lifetime.

When I began putting these memories down on paper I found myself in need of a few more angels. Once again my cousin, Rod Griffin, came to the rescue with his reminiscences of this coast. George and Nellie Powell welcomed me to their library, as did Robert Christensen, Nellie Jeffery, and Katie Thompson. Norman Erikson told me the history of the lonely pilings that are all that remain of bustling fishing outports, and Alan Luoma remembered Granite Bay as it was. Joe Christensen, in his role as prospector, was another angel. When I needed information about the history of Ucluelet, my cousin Marjorie Dufour and pioneer Mary Baird were invaluable. In the early stages of this work my writing friend, Joe Pidutti, wielded his red pencil and urged me toward some degree of organization. And once again my capable editor, Audrey McClellan, came cheerfully to the task of tidying up the loose bits. But the final blessing goes to my publisher, Rodger Touchie, for his encouragement and for his sense of vision.

Bibliography

Andersen, Doris. *The Columbia is Coming!* Sidney, BC: Gray's Publishing Ltd., 1982.

Blanchet, M. Wylie. *The Curve of Time*. Sidney, BC: Gray's Publishing Ltd., 1968.

Boating News (a monthly newspaper issued by Donald Tyrell during the 1970s and 1980s that documented events in B.C. boating, including race results).

Cameron, June. *Destination Cortez Island*. Surrey, BC: Heritage House Publishing Co., 1999.

Chappell, John. *Cruising Beyond Desolation Sound*. Vancouver, BC: Naikoon Marine, 1979.

Fulghum, Robert. *Uh Oh*. New York, NY: Villard Press, 1991.

Furlong, Marjorie and Virginia Pill. *Edible? Incredible!* Tacoma, WA: Erco, Inc., 1973.

Golby, Humphrey and Shirley Hewett. *Swiftsure: The First 50 Years 1930-1980*. Victoria, BC: Lightship Press, 1980.

Gould, Ed. *Logging: British Columbia's Logging History*. Saanichton, BC: Hancock House Publishers, 1975.

Harold, Hughina. *Totem Poles and Tea*. Surrey, BC: Heritage House Publishing Co., 1996.

Iglauer, Edith. *Fishing with John*. Madeira Park, BC: Harbour Publishing Co., 1988.

Isnor, D.E., E.G. Stephens, and D.E. Watson. *Edge of Discovery*. Campbell River, BC: Ptarmigan Press, 1989.

McKelvie, B.A. *Tales of Conflict*. Surrey, BC: Heritage House Publishing

Co., 1985.

Morrisette, Gloria. Self-published account of her childhood on B.C.'s coast. Available from author at 25007 Morrisette Place, Maple Ridge, BC V2W 1G8.

Museum at Campbell River. *The Raincoast Kitchen*. Madeira Park, BC: Harbour Publishing Co., 1996.

Nicholson, George S.W. *Vancouver Island's West Coast 1762-1962*. Victoria: Morriss Printing, 1962.

Pacific Yachting magazine.

Paterson, T.W. *Ghost Town Trails of Vancouver Island*. Langley, BC: Stagecoach Publishing, 1975.

Peterson, Lester R. *The Cape Scott Story*. Vancouver, BC: Mitchell Press, 1974.

Pinkerton, Kathrene. *Three's a Crew*. Ganges, BC: Horsdal and Schubart Publishers Ltd., 1991.

Underhill, J.E. *Northwestern Wild Berries*. Surrey, BC: Hancock House, 1980.

Walbran, Captain John T. *British Columbia Coast Names, 1592-1906*. Vancouver, BC: J.J. Douglas, 1971.

Wild, Paula. *Sointula: Island Utopia*. Madeira Park, BC: Harbour Publishing Co., 1995.

Index

Addenbroke lighthouse 196

Ahclakerho Channel 163

Ahousat 110–111

Alert Bay 150

Alison Sound 141–143, 145

Allard Arm 209, 211

Allison Harbour 138–140, 146

Allons 90

Anchor Cove 163

Anderson, Doris 133

Anglican Coast Mission 133, 182

Ann Island 214, 216, 218

Anne Island 204

Antle, John 133

Appleseeds 149, 196

Ashbridge, P.B. 101

Bachen, Bob 206

Bad News 52

Bagheera 14

Baird, Mary 113–114, 115

Ballenas Island race 49–52

Barkley Sound 77–79, 112, 115

Barrier Islands 94

Battle Bay 93–94, 112

BC Packers 200

BC Troller 129

Beaver 122

Beaver Harbour 122, 156, 188

Belize Inlet 141, 143

Big Bay 174

Biggin-Pound, Jack 78, 112, 115

Biggin-Pound, Nora 78, 112, 115

Billy Goat Bay 183, 184

Blackfish Sound 171

Blackney Passage 150, 185

Blair Island 196

Blanchet, Muriel Wylie 131, 144

Blunden Harbour 147, 148

Boas, Kay 24–25

Boas, Rollo 23–26, 220

boat racing: calculating finishes 61; clubs
    30; ratings 31; starts 48

Bodega Island 105–106

Boswell Inlet 162, 165, 211

Bowen Island 51

British Columbia Coast Names 119

Brown's Bay 178

Brown's Sawmill 129

Brydon Channel 204

Bull Harbour 84, 125, 126–128

Bunsby Islands 94

Butler, June 43

California Packing Corporation 98

Cameron, Alan Douglas 9, 12–20, 23–
    27, 30, 39–42, 66, 78, 84

Cameron, Ian 66, 82, 154

Cameron, June 14, 86, 161, 221: early
    boating 9; buys *Saffron* 14–15; sets
    goals 26, 27, 220–221; Power
    Squadron courses 27; agrees to race
    Saffron 28; first club sailpast 30–
    31; single-handed sailing 31–34,

36–38, 66, 115, 207; single-handed race 31, 36–38, 42, 76; all-female crew 47–48, 51, 52, 60, 64, 73, 77; buys *Papillion* 73; sells *Saffron* 73; and family 14, 16, 18, 25, 81–82, 84, 154; deafness 80; moves to Vancouver 82; retires from teaching 82; Vancouver Island circumnavigation 82, 83–117; women on boats 60, 75, 82, 153; anchoring technique 152; docking technique 205; navigation 17, 44, 51, 57, 76, 96, 115; art 80–81, 118, 124, 127, 175; paintings 21, 22, 125, 162, 165, 176, 199, 212; writing 122, 127, 153, 175, 208.

Cameron, Trudy 14, 30, 47, 67, 124

Campbell River 176–177

Canadian Packing Corporation 99

Canoe Landing 91

Cape Beale 115

Cape Caution 141, 154, 159, 188, 207, 220

Cape Cook 90, 91

Cape Flattery 108

Cape Scott 84, 85, 86, 87–88

Cape Scott 87, 88

The Cape Scott Story 88

Cardena 191

Cardew, Carol 77

Caroline Lake 211

Cascade Harbour 129

Catala Island 96, 103

Catchalot Inlet 96

Cattle Island 124

Ceepeecee 97–101, 105

Chappell, John 68, 140, 169

Charlotte Bay 146

Chatham Point lighthouse 182

Chelosin 179

Chettleburgh, Peter 52

Christensen, Joe 91, 130

Clallam Bay 45, 58

Clam Bay 159

Clayoquot Sound 110–111

Clear Passage 96

Cluster Reefs 214

coast guard 126

Collins, Frank 97–100, 105

Collins, Linda 97–100, 105

Columbia Coast Mission 23

The Columbia is Coming! 133

Comox 15, 17

Convoy Passage 204

Copeland, Andy 14, 48

Cormorant Island 150

Cortes Bay 18, 118, 168, 176

Cortes Island 9, 17–19, 22–23, 66

Cougar Inlet 140–141

Cox Island 85

Crowe, Al 74

Cruising Beyond Desolation Sound 68, 140

The Curve of Time 144

Dale, Bill 113

Darby Channel 189–191, 196

Dawson's Landing 191, 196, 205–206, 209

de Cevallos, Ciriaco 104

Deer Island 123

Dent Rapids 173

Desolation Sound 39, 66, 118

Destination Cortez Island 10, 13

Dibben, Kate 133

Dickson Island 168

Disney, Charlie 172

Donaldson, Sven 36, 45–47, 50, 175

Donnelly, Aldyen 48

Donnelly, Bill 45–46, 48

Drake, Francis 144

Draney Inlet 175, 188, 192, 195, 207–208, 210–213, 214

Drury Inlet 169–170
Duncanby Landing 193–195, 208–209, 213
Dunsmuir, Robert 123
Duval Point 131

Echo Bay 132
Edible? Incredible! 92
Edna Island 204
Effingham Island 78, 112, 115
Egg Island 159, 214
Egret Plume 11 210
Esperanza Inlet 96–102
Esperanza Mission 97, 100–101
Estevan Point 109
Estevan Point lighthouse 105

Fairmile Passage 198, 204
Fast, Diane 82, 83–86, 89–98, 100–112, 119, 127
Finnie, Dick 19
Fish Egg Inlet 175, 196, 199
Fish Trap Bay 197
Fishermans Bay 88
Fishhook Bay 212, 213
fishing industry 95, 99–100, 114, 125, 128, 131, 158, 159, 166–167, 176, 189, 190–192, 195, 200–201, 203, 204, 215
Fishing with John 104
Fitzhugh Sound 198
FitzJames, Mike 15, 43–44, 174
Fly Basin 219
Ford Cove 12
Fort Rupert 119, 122–123
Fraser, George 113–114
Fraser River Lightship race 75
Friendly Cove 106, 108, 109
Frisk, Eleanor 48, 51, 54–55, 61, 67, 68, 70, 77, 78, 79, 119, 151
Fury Cove 189, 190, 205

Gavin, Fraser 168
Gavin, Georgina 168
Gay Passage 94
Ghost Town Trails of Vancouver Island 104
Gillard Rapids 173–174
Gissing, Cliff 104
Godkin, Norman 128–129
God's Pocket 159
Goletas Cannery 129
Goose Bay Cannery 191
Goose Islands 118
Gordon Lake 164
Gowlland Harbour 176
Granite Bay 179–182
Grave Island 135, 136, 187
Green Island 198, 199
Green Point Rapids 171
Greenway Sound Resort 170–171
Grider, Wendy 77
Grief Point 83
Griffin, George (brother) 18, 32, 77, 85, 96, 100, 104, 112, 113, 114
Griffin, George (father) 16, 25, 81–82, 84
Griffin, Marjorie 15, 16, 18, 25
Griffin, Rod 20, 128, 129–130, 138–139
Griffin, Sharleen 48, 67
Growler Cove 184

Hakai Pass 196
Hansen, Lily 151, 184
Hansen, Lorna 151, 184
Hansen, Ole 151, 184
Hanson Island 150
Harold, Hughina 133, 135
Harriet Point 145
Harris Island 220
Hastings Mills and Trading Company 180
Hayes, Art 18, 185

Hayes, Bob 18
Hayes, Dave 209, 210
Hayes, Frank 18
Hayes, Mimi 209–210
Heather Civic Marina 28
Helmcken Island 119, 183
Helmcken, John 119
Hickey Cove 158, 164
Hill, Gordie 54
Hill, Meg 54, 55, 57, 58
Hole in the Wall Rapids 40
Holmes Point 144
Holsinger, Paul 72–73, 118, 119, 135, 139, 168, 179, 196, 200
Hope Island 84, 125
Horn Point 173
Hornby Island 12
Hot Springs Cove 109–110, 111
Hudson's Bay Company 119, 122–123
Hunt, Mrs. George 123
Hunt, Robert 123
Hurricane Island 204

Iglauer, Edith 104
Illahie Inlet 198
Insley, Al 200
Insley, Bev 200
Insley, Kate 200

James, Michelle 47, 55, 64–65, 67, 70, 72, 73, 77
Jammer 199
Jeffery, Barry 132
Jeffery, Nellie 18, 67, 84, 131–133, 135, 137
Joe Cove 171
Johnson, Axel 209–210, 211
Johnson Bay 191, 192–193
Johnstone Strait 119, 176, 182–183
Jones Cove 159, 160, 166, 220
Juan de Fuca Strait 77, 115. See also

Swiftsure race
Juno 73–76, 77, 81, 89, 110, 122, 142, 143, 152, 164, 165, 212

Kalect Islet 125–126, 159
Karn, W. 114
Kerr and Dumaresque logging camp 139
Kildidt Sound 203
Kittyhawk Group 204
Klaskino Anchorage 90
Knight Inlet 68, 133, 176, 187
Koeye River 200
Kwakume Inlet 199, 200
Kyuquot 94
Kyuquot Sound 95

Lancaster Rocks 204
Lasqueti Island 71
Lasseter Bay 141
Lefeaux, Bob 37, 50, 52
logging 95, 106, 114, 129, 138–139, 165, 170, 180, 182, 184, 210
Loran navigation device 76, 79
Loran Passage 214
Loumar 9
Lucky Jim Gold Mine 181
Lumeral 162, 163
Luoma, Alan 180
Luoma, Alfred 180
Luoma, Emil 180

Malahat 129
Malcolm Island 187
Mamalilaculla 68–70, 84, 133–135, 186–187
Manley Island 203
Maple Bay regatta 72
Margaret Bay 158, 162
Maude Island 178
McBride Bay 162, 164
McGruer, Lorne 43, 45, 47

McNeill, W.H. 123
Melanie Cove 19, 20
Miles Inlet 166, 189, 220, 221
Millerd Brothers fish camp 159
mining 123, 172, 181
Minstrel Island 68
Mitlenatch Island 17
Morrisette, Gloria 128
Muirhead Islands 170
Murray, Gladys 80

Nahwitti Bar 84–85, 122, 126, 128, 153
Nakwakto Rapids 139, 140, 144
Nalau Passage 202–203
Namu 196, 200–202, 204
Nebo 76
New Vancouver 135–137
Newton, John 109
Nigei Island 159
Nootka Island 106–108
Nootka Sound 99
Nootka Trail 108
Norman Islet 127
Northwestern Wild Berries 92
Nuchatlitz 102–103
Nugent Sound 144
Numas Island 168

O'Brien, Kathleen 133
Octopus Islands 40
Okisollos Rapids 40
Otter Cove 182

Pachena 109
Pacific Handicap Racing Fleet (PHRF) 31
Pacific Yachting 52, 122, 127, 153, 163, 175, 197, 199, 208
Papillion 73. See also *Juno*.
Paterson, T.W. 104

Patrol Passage 204
Pender Harbour 72
Penrose Island 189
Perry, Mary Amanda 208–210, 213
Peterson, Grace 169
Peterson, Henry 169
Peterson, Henry 87, 88
Peterson, Lester 88
Peterson, Nora 87
Phillips Arm 171
pilchards 98–99
Pinkerton, Kathrene 123, 131
Port Eliza 96–97
Port Eliza 97
Port Hardy 121, 124, 125, 128, 131, 158, 188, 189
Port McNeill 131
Port Neville 120, 151–152, 184
Port Renfrew 116
Prideaux Haven 19–20
Pulteney Point 121

Quadra Island 179–180, 182
Qualicum wind 13
Queen Charlotte Islands 72
Queen Charlotte Sound 168
Queen Charlotte Strait 138, 149
Queen Cove 96

Raepple, Wally 72, 73
Read Island 39
Redonda Island 19
Reilly, Anne 149–150, 152–153, 181, 188–189, 191–198, 200, 202–207
Reilly, Chris 207
Renfrew, Karen 54, 55, 58, 60
Retreat Passage 133
Richmond Bay 169
Rivers Inlet 85, 127, 175, 188, 189, 191, 209, 214

Robert Arm 211, 212
Robinson, Desmond 97
Robinson, Tony 97
Robson Bight 184
rock paintings 143–144, 145
Rolling Roadstead 96
Royal Navy Sailing Association 30, 38, 109
Royal Vancouver Yacht Club (Royal Van) 29, 48
Royal Victoria Yacht Club 62
Rugged Point 95, 96

Saffron 9, 14, 18, 28, 31, 32, 40, 44, 51, 55, 61, 62–63, 73, 152, 205
San Josef Bay 86–88
San Josef River 88
Scarlett Point lighthouse 159
Scholberg 129
Schooner Channel 140
Schwartzenberg Lagoon 144
Scotty Bay 71
Sea Otter Cove 86, 88
Secret Cove 71
Seymour Inlet 138–139, 141, 145–146, 166
Seymour Narrows 119–120, 176–179
Seymour, Skip 195, 209, 211
Shantyman's Christian Association 100
Shaula 104
Shell Island 124
Shoal Bay 171–173
Shushartie Bay 128–130
Silva Bay Layover race 34–36
Skeeter II 129
Slingsby Channel 140
Small Basin 182
Small Inlet 182
Smelt Bay 17, 67
Smith Inlet 154, 156, 162, 163, 175
Smith Sound 154, 162, 163, 214–219

Sointula 120–121, 187
Solander Island 90–91
Southern Straits race 43–45, 63–64, 76
Southgate Group 138, 140, 147
Souvenir Passage 198
Specialty Yachts 14
Spider Island 196, 202
Spitfire Channel 204
sport fishing 68, 114, 166, 168, 204
Squitty Bay 71
Sterling, Malcolm 47
Steyn, Douw 45
Storch, Gerry 28–29, 31–32, 34, 35–36, 43, 46, 74
Storch Sails 44, 46
Strait of Georgia 11, 13, 39, 173
Stuart Island 26
Sullivan Bay 168, 170
Summers Bay 143
Surge Narrows 39
Surprise Island 95
Susie 154–157, 159, 160–162, 169, 171, 185, 193, 205, 207, 211, 218–219, 220, 221
Sutil Point 128
Swiftsure race 56: Juan de Fuca division 45–46, 54–62, 76
Swiftsure: The First Fifty Years 62
Sydney Inlet 110

Table Island 214, 216–217
Tahsis Inlet 98, 107, 109
Tatnall Reef 85, 128
Taylor Bay 207–208
Templar Channel 111
Texada Island 71
Theodosia Inlet 20–21, 22
Thomas Crosby IV 210
Timmerman, John 62
Ting 47
Tofino 111, 114

Totem Poles and Tea 133
Traill, Barbara 35–36
Turn Island 182–183

Ucluelet 77, 111–114
Underhill Island 203
Union Island 95
Union Steamship Company 128, 130, 172, 179, 191
United Church Mission 210

Vancouver, George 144
Vancouver Island: gold 104, 114; northern tip 84, 91; outer coast 92, 94, 96, 99, 109, 111
Victoria Shipyard 129
Village Channel 187
Village Island 133
Von Donop Inlet 22–23, 26, 174

Wadhams 191–192
Waiatt Bay 40, 182
Walbran Island 207, 210

Walbran, John 119
Walker, Margery 137–138, 140–149, 156, 158–159, 162–166, 176–185, 187
Wardell, Dennis 109
Warner Bay 145
Waysash Inlet 164
Wells Passage 168–169
West Vancouver Yacht Club 29
Western Forest Products 171
Whaletown 23, 25
Whirlpool Rapids 119, 171
whisker pole 13
Whiterock Passage 41
Williams, Deb 78
Winter Harbour 88–89, 97
Wood Duck 73
Wynne, Elaine 82

Yuculta Rapids 26, 68, 173

Zeballos 102, 103, 104–105

Quality Books of Adventure
and History Along the
B.C. Coast Available from Heritage House

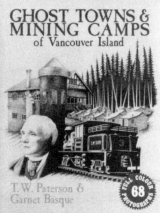

*Grizzlies
in Their Backyard*
Beth Day
ISBN 1-895811-16-3
$14.95

*Ghost Towns and Mining Camps
of Vancouver Island*
T.W. Paterson & Garnet Basque
ISBN 1-895811-80-5
$21.95

*Totem Poles
and Tea*
Hughina Harold
ISBN 1-895811-11-2
$17.95

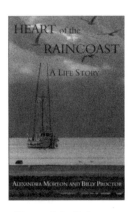

Heart of the Raincoast
Alexandra Morton
and Billy Proctor
ISBN 0-920663-61-3
$15.95

*Glyphs
and Gallows*
Peter Johnson
ISBN 1-895811-94-5
$18.95

*Upcoast
Summers*
Beth Hill
ISBN 0-920663-01-X
$12.95

ISBN 1-895811-68-6
$17.95

"This has to be one of the most important books about life up the coast ... the history of the early coastal settlement is there as well, giving insight into the challenges, the dangers, and disappointments early pioneers faced ... I was amazed at the extent of the knowledge of small-boat engines Cameron displays ... It is all between these pages, the dropping-in on neighbours, dances, details like the number of students needed for a school, how a homestead was built ... I highly recommend this book. I can't imagine anyone not getting something worthwhile from it ... Maybe *Destination Cortez Island* will make Canadians realize there is also an up-the-West-Cast lifestyle. Buy it, read it, enjoy."

Kelsey McLeod
Vancouver Historical Society

June Cameron and Susie at Smelt Bay, Cortes Island, with her cruiser at anchor.

June Cameron grew up in Vancouver and spent her childhood summers on Cortes Island. Since the mid-1970s she has been sailing up and down the coast, and at the age of 65 she moved onto a small displacement cruiser in order to do research for her books. She currently lives on board with her small dog. Her first book, *Destination Cortez Island*, was a memoir of those summers on Cortes and a tribute to the pioneers of the Desolation Sound area.